Praise for *Raising Intuitive Children*:

"*Raising Intuitive Children* fulfills an urgent need in teaching parents how to nurture our children's most important sense: their intuition. It is at home, from their parents, where children either learn to trust, express, and follow their natural wisdom, leading to fulfilled and peaceful lives, or to dismiss their intuition, thus losing their way, their joy, and their Spirit. A must read for all parents, as all children are inherently intuitive."

—**Sonia Choquette**, author of *The Intuitive Spark*

"Our society is changing and the paradigms of childcare as well as the rearing of intuitive children must sway from archaic standards to a more realistic perspective. *Raising Intuitive Children* gives parents excellent explanations with true-life stories that first brings normalcy to what has previously been viewed as a phenomenon, and then provides a terrific skill set for parents and caregivers alike. *Raising Intuitive Children* is a must read for anyone having anything to do with the children of now."

—**Meg Blackburn Losey**, PhD, author of *Conversations with the Children of Now* and *The Children of Now*

"Wow, if only my parents had read Tara and Caron's profound and deep advice! As a 22 year-old, I struggle constantly to explain to parents what kids are going through and how to reach them, yet Tara and Caron's warmth, honesty, and open reflections bring to light many issues that generations of youth have been struggling with—but have never been able to express."

—**Vanessa Van Petten**, teen author of *You're Grounded!* and creator of OnTeensToday.com

"This major work provides effective strategies for nurturing the intuitive child's personal style of relating to the world, an absolute necessity for character excellence and success in their purpose."

—**Kendall Gammon**, retired, former member of the Kansas City Chiefs, author of *Life's a Snap: Building on the Past to Improve Your Future* and *Game Plan: Leadership Lessons from the Best of the NFL*

"I was deeply moved by the anticipated focus of this work. The informed use, respect, and honoring of our intuitive selves has the most potential of bringing about larger societal shifts when support and value of this way of being is first present in the home. It is imperative that we do all we can to support our children in developing their gifts, and *Raising Intuitive Children* is a bold and loving directive on how to do just that. "

—**Dr. Idara E. Bassey**, attorney/intuitive and host of Sedona Talk Radio's "Everyday Divinity"

"The time has finally come to support and encourage the intuitive children of the world and Tara Paterson and Caron Goode do it brilliantly. This is a book that every parent, who even thinks his or her child may be intuitive, must have. *Raising Intuitive Children* is *the* catalyst for making huge, positive changes in intuitive children's lives and the family as a whole."

—**Linda Salazar**, suthor of *Awaken the Genie Within*

Raising Intuitive Children

Guide Your Children to Know
and Trust Their Gifts

By Caron B. Goode, EdD, and Tara Paterson

New Page Books
A Division of The Career Press, Inc.
Franklin Lakes, NJ

Raising Intuitive Children
Edited by Kate Henches
Typeset by Gina Talucci
Cover design by Howard Grossman/12E Designs
Drawings and charts by Patricia Rausch
Printed in the U.S.A.

To order this title, please call toll-free 1-800-CAREER-1 (NJ and Canada: 201-848-0310) to order using VISA or MasterCard, or for further information on books from Career Press.

The Career Press, Inc., 3 Tice Road, PO Box 687,
Franklin Lakes, NJ 07417
www.careerpress.com
www.newpagebooks.com

Library of Congress Cataloging-in-Publication Data
Goode, Caron B.
    Raising intuitive children : guide your children to know and trust
their gifts / by
    Caron B. Goode and Tara Paterson.
            p. cm.
Includes bibliographical references and index.
ISBN 978-1-60163-051-3
1. Parenting. 2. Child development. 3. Intuition. 4. Exceptional children. I.
            Paterson, Tara. II. Title.

HQ755.8.G667 2009
649'.1--dc22

                                                                2008054047

Dedication and Acknowledgments

Caron dedicates this to her husband:

To Tom, the wings beneath my wind—thank you!

Tara dedicates this book to the following people in her life:

To my supportive husband, Chris; thank you so much for grounding me all these years while I focused on developing my inner and outer passion. It hasn't been an easy journey, but I am blessed to have a husband who knows the intuitive value our children bring to the world.

To my children, Adam, Caden, and Kaylee, you are my beacons of light. I am blessed to walk this journey with you and share the same heart space on this planet. There aren't enough pages in this book to describe the undying love and pride I feel for each of you.

To my daughter, Avery Rae, who will be with us by the time this book is printed. Yet another of God's blessings to the world.

Caron

I am grateful for the Guidance that directs the passion and the purpose of this book in its mission to empower the families with intuitive members. Thank you, Tom, for his endless hours of reading and helpful suggestions. Deep appreciation for you, Tara, for stepping into this long-term relationship with passion, idealism, and joy. Deep gratitude also goes to Devra, who dances with words, and for believing in the work.

Tara

It has been an uphill battle to bring the content of this book to the world, but I could not have done it without the inspiration and support of so many wonderful, intuitive people in my life.

To Dr. Caron Goode, my coauthor, mentor, and friend. You have been such a resource for support and education, and without you and your wonderful husband Tom, I would not know the intuitive person I am today—my deepest appreciation.

To Linda Salazar, my spiritual coach and friend. You have taught me so many techniques for managing my energy and my life. Without your sage words of advice, I wouldn't remember "not" to create a story about everything. Thank you.

To my dad, who is no longer with us. You taught me strength, unconditional love, how to live in the moment, and, most of all, that the heart is all that matters. *"What we have once enjoyed and deeply loved we can never lose, for all that we deeply love becomes a part of us."* —Helen Keller

To my mom, my greatest challenge, my deepest source of joy, and my friend. We have had our highs and our lows, but the lessons you have taught me have made me the compassionate, caring, loving person I am today. Without you, I would not know my deepest self. My greatest appreciation goes to you, because, without you, I wouldn't know the depth of my soul.

Contents

Foreword

Intuitive intelligence is an innate part of who we are. It is a very real aspect of our awareness in any given moment.

Our intuition tells us things beyond our everyday perceptions. It tells us what people are really saying, and what their motivation is. Our intuition often tells us what is next, what to do or not to do, and even when other people are thinking about us. Our intuition tells us when we are safe and when we are not.

It is a vital aspect to our sensory experiences. It is a sense with which we are born that is most often denied.

Using our intuitive intelligence means being in tune with all of creation, intentionally letting down our guards and allowing ourselves to become open to the infinite possibilities that are available to us in the form of awareness.

The problem is that most of us aren't connecting or listening, mostly because we don't know how to. We are afraid of what we don't understand and we don't want to be singled out as being different. But we are not different. As the authors point out, all of us are intuitive, and have the capacity to develop these vital awareness skills.

Currently we are experiencing a leap in the evolution of human consciousness. More and more people are spontaneously utilizing intuition on a regular basis. It is my belief, my intrinsic knowing, that all of us are capable of tapping into the intuitive gifts that are within us.

Many of our children, whom I call the children of now, are coming into our world with undeniable attributes that are intuitive and even beyond that, having a greatly connected sensitivity to other people, our environment, and everything in between. Because of this, our new generation needs parents who are willing to set aside their sense of having to be normal and acceptable, of being in control, fitting into a preconceived norm, and who are willing to utilize their higher intuitive nature to ascertain the needs of their children. It is time to move out of our familiar boxes and step into the possibilities that are available to us.

The bottom line is that the old rules don't apply. We are on the brink—and soon to become immersed in—an entirely new paradigm of parenting and social development. If we are to know how to intuit what our children need, we must overcome our fears of the unknown and take an honest look at the possibilities beyond those old rules. To do this, we must first understand how our intuitive nature presents in our children and ourselves and further, how to apply it to real life.

With the combined expertise of authors Dr. Caron Goode and Tara Paterson, *Raising Intuitive Children* brings to the reader a terrific set of tools for the understanding and the application of intuitive intelligence that can enhance the familial experience from this day forward. Imagine the possibilities of development in our children when they are no longer stifled by rules and parenting guidelines that no longer make sense.

With thoughtful intentional intuitive parenting, our children will become a generation of openly aware people. They'll be unafraid of the truth or will express it because they have been taught that the truth is just fine and that by using their intuition life becomes an unlimited and amazing journey with infinite possibilities left only to their imagining.

Imagine what the children of now will do with our world with the freedom to use their gifts and with parents who really get it.

—Meg Blackburn Losey, PhD
author of the international best-sellers,
The Children of Now and *Conversations With the Children of Now*
(New Page Books, 2006 and 2008)

Introduction

Welcome to *Raising Intuitive Children*. Parenting in general calls for great attention and commitment. Parenting children with intuition also involves practicing awareness and trust. You must be able to trust your inner knowing; at some point you may have to overcome labels and judgments. As a child, were you told that you were "overly or too sensitive" by the teachers and adults around you? Perhaps no one understood that you had special needs. Even less likely was their awareness that you had special gifts.

This book is written for *all* intuitively gifted children and their parents, so that, together they may enjoy better communication, greater success, and deeper love and understanding. It is also for all of your family members to enable a mutually supportive and harmonious family unit.

Intuition is finally recognized as a natural intelligence and not a curse on the creative or aware children who possess this natural attribute. Yet nurturing the potential of an intuitive child is not something parents have been taught.

Raising Intuitive Children teaches you how to recognize and nurture the intuitive child, a book for you to keep on your shelf as a reference guide. It gives you the needed tools to empower your children to manage their worlds rather than being disabled by them. An easy read, you will learn what to do and how to do it.

Helping those once called indigo, a crystal or new earth child demands different approaches. You'll learn which attributes of psychic perceptions and spiritual awareness your child has and how best to work with her. You'll also become part of a growing, global network of people interested in the gifts these children bring us.

Are these children more evolved? How do they differ from other children? Are their abilities inherited? Do they need medication? These are just some of the questions we, as parents of intuitive children, have asked ourselves.

In the past four decades, we have observed the rise in children's measured intelligence scores and the classes for the gifted that have opened to accommodate them. Today, intuitive intelligence has risen to the forefront and children with intuitive gifts may be as many as a fourth of all children. These children are open and connected to non-physical worlds beyond those of normal human perception. More aware and sensitive, they learn and process in ways that are different from how most schools teach. Yet there are new tools.

Parents today know about whole-brain learning and whole-child parenting. In 2000, RIC author Caron Goode wrote *Nurture Your Child's Gift* (Beyond Words, 2000) and described the model for parenting the whole child with instruction on finding your child's natural core genius.

In this book, the core genius topic is the intuitive intelligence continuum. We explore thoroughly how this natural intelligence interacts with other intelligences to produce unique talent streams. We identify and discuss strategies for the creative intuitive, empathic intuitive, psychic intuitive, and spiritual intuitive.

Intuitive children often have an intuitive parent, many of whom don't realize their talents. Tara Paterson discovered her intuition in adulthood, but her mother had it all along. Perhaps you've had an experience similar to Kathy's, whose intuitive intelligence was natural to her.

A mother's intuition

Kathy, a 56-year-old grandmother at the time she was interviewed for this book, recalled two events she named "mother's intuition." Studies show that humans can perceive events in slow motion during the final seconds before car wrecks, airplane crashes, or other situations that pose a real threat. Intuitive intelligence is heightened when we sense and respond to imminent danger.

Kathy was a young mother, sitting at her breakfast table, watching the birds flutter at the bird feeder and her five-year-old daughter playing in the yard. A rock wall about two feet high separated the family's driveway from the yard. Kathy's daughter climbed on to the wall and practiced walking on her imaginary balance beam.

Kathy's sixth sense kicked in. She suddenly flew out of her seat, rushed out the door, and ran across the yard in time to catch her daughter in her arms as she fell off the wall. Kathy amazed herself with her speed in reaching her daughter before she hit the hard earth. To this day she would swear the angels carried her; she believes she could not have made it to her daughter in time.

Yet she acted immediately and in time to prevent a potentially harmful event. What caused Kathy to move so quickly? How did she know to act immediately and how did she manage to make it out of the house and run across the yard to catch her daughter at the moment of her fall?

Research on intuition

Our mind and bodies are hardwired for intuition, as some recent research discovered. In 2004, The Journal of Alternative and Complementary Medicine *reported the study results of "Electrophysiological Evidence of Intuition: Part 1. The Surprising Role of the Heart." The reported results follow:*

"The main findings in relation to the heart's role in intuitive perception are: (1) the heart appears to receive and respond to intuitive information; (2) a significantly greater heart rate deceleration occurred prior to future emotional stimuli compared to calm stimuli; (3) there were significant gender differences in the processing of pre-stimulus information."[1]

One of our most influential tools for parenting is the power of our intuition, our inner sense sometimes called a voice of knowing. At another time, Kathy was enjoying her end-of-the-day routine after putting her three children to bed. She liked to sit alone at night, read a good book, and enjoy the solitude. One night, she felt something touch the back of her neck. She turned to see what it was when a voice in her head told her to check her infant son. She got up immediately and went to his room to see that as he lay in his crib he was not breathing. Later at a symposium, she learned that her son was a prime candidate for SIDS. Sudden Infant Death Syndrome would have claimed another life if she hadn't trusted the voice she heard and taken action. The intuitive traits that Kathy showed were

- being self-aware of feelings and perceptions.
- trusting instinctive feelings—even when the outcome was unknown by the logical mind.
- feeling connected to the feelings of others.

Different drummers, different learning

Dancing through life as an intuitive means our children will discover and move to their internal rhythms, not always to other's expectations. Yet intuition presents itself differently in each child, as does any talent.

The first question at our conferences is, "Aren't all children intuitive?" Our answer is, "Yes, all have the capacity for intuition because we are all human and share the same biochemistry for processing information."

And, *how* children develop their intuition is more about their interests or strengths. The following chart names the natural intelligences that all human being possess to some degree.

- Physical intelligence.
- Mental-creative intelligence.
- Emotional-social intelligence.
- Intuitive intelligence.
- Spiritual intelligence.

Pairing these intelligences with intuitive intelligence, we clearly see the varied intuitive gifts and needs of our children, the hot topics for your reading!

Natural Intelligences	Plus Intuitive Intelligence =
Physical Prowess Enhanced by Intuitive Intelligence	
Physical	*Learns by doing, has exceptional kinesthesia, motor skills, sense of timing, and movement with the body.*
Creative, Inspired Intuitive	
Mental-Creative	*Inspired, inventive, creative, follows inner music, ideas, and actions motivated by internal genius. Can daydream, be distracted, learns to focus, and learns through experimentation.*
Empathic Intuitive	
Emotional-Social	*Reads others, feels others, defines self in relation to others. Needs boundaries, emotional management skills, self-identification, and confidence.*
Psychic Intuitive	
Intuitive	*Expanded awareness of the nonphysical worlds or subtle energy fields through receptors in the biochemistry. Exhibits talents of subtle knowing, hearing, seeing, telepathy, and other talents.*
Spiritual Intuitive	
Spiritual	*Intuition serves kids with spiritual intelligence as the doorway and interpreter to connection with inner worlds.*

Intuitive intelligence is the new kid on the block. The parenting suggestions presented support intuitive children in several ways.

- Helping children identify, understand, and use their talent.
- Helping children verify their intuition with their logic, if needed.
- Enabling children to negotiate a logic-based, intellectual culture by using their intuitive feelings or hunches.
- Strengthening children's self-trust for their greatest successes.

Enjoy the read and find wisdom!

1

Whole Child: A Winning Body and Mind Combination

True enjoyment comes from activity of the mind and exercise of the body; the two are united.

—Alexander von Humboldt

Energy, body, and mind

Science has shown many truths about life processes. One is that all life processes are energy phenomena. Energy creates matter and matter changes back into energy. The growth, maintenance, and activities of body and mind depend on energy to live and operate. In this chapter, you'll find out how to help children manage their energy and what some of their energy needs are. Then the following chapters focus on these needs of the child whose core talents are in the realm of intuitive intelligence.

Classical medical sciences describe the body as having different types of energy that work together. They ensure that mind and body live optimally or at their best. Specifically, the different types of energy are called etheric, mental, and emotional energies.

Etheric energy—Think of etheric energy as the electro-magnetic energy field radiated by the body. Etheric energy affects the physical functioning of the body. The health of the body's cells, tissues, and organs depend on it. Etheric energy helps hearts beat, stomachs digest food, and cells repair. Toxins in our environment can cause etheric energy to be less effective. Emotional traumas can also damage it.

Mental energy influences our spiritual viewpoint. This energy helps us gain perspective on our place in life and helps us balance the other activities of body and mind. Mental energy can help children cope with excessive stress through logic or creative imagination. Using mental energy, children can imagine that they are in the "big picture" of life. It serves as a foundation for faith and answers children's questions about their existence. Some of these questions are:

- What is my life's purpose?
- What is death?
- Who am I?
- What am I doing here on earth?
- What things do I need to live well and happily?

We use mental energy to think and feel security. We gain insight into the mysteries of life and how we should act toward others. Some children may not know about spiritual values. If they do not, they become insecure and uncertain about positive values. They may feel ambivalent about their life experiences and making decisions.

Emotional energy controls our thoughts and emotions. We experience it in a subjective way. Emotional energy forms the basis of personal character. It also directs our own definitions of pain and pleasure. Emotional energy is the foundation for:

- Thought processes.
- How we gain knowledge.
- Emotional relationships.

In our society, emotional energy has to work harder in many children than the other types of energy. Children sometimes live in bad homes or other abusive situations. Mom or dad may pressure their kids to succeed in school or in sports. The media constantly pressures kids to buy things. Peers may put pressure on a child to fit in. And schools expect maturity, too. Students must achieve academically and behave socially. Many children are not ready to meet all the demands placed on them.

Emotional and etheric types of energy are opposites. The more we feel emotional, the more we use our emotional energy, which means we have less etheric energy left over to cope with our physical needs. Because of emotional stress, we may suffer from physical problems.

Etheric energy is important. We may not have enough of it if we are over stimulated emotionally, because emotional energy scatters or disperses. This is especially true if we react emotionally over and over again throughout a long period of time.

If we do not have enough etheric energy, we can get tired and be erratic. Our appetite may go up or down, or we may not sleep well. Our bodies may feel tense and tired. We may also lack enough etheric energy if there are too many toxins in the body. We may feel unwell and lack the energy to live active and fulfilling lives.

A **spiritual perspective** can increase your stamina and vitality and improves etheric, emotional, and mental energies. We share it when talking about the "big" questions in life with our children. A spiritual foundation helps us and our children balance the different parts of our lives. It gives us a framework for understanding adversity or distress, illness, or death. A spiritual perspective will help our etheric, mental, and emotional types of energy work well and stay in proper proportion to one another.

The connection between the body and the mind

Within a human being, the body's organs connect directly to the mind. The body and mind work together, and each reflects the health of the other. But the connection is even closer than that. The organ system expresses what is going on in the mind. Your mental state is an emotional reflection of specific organ systems.

Throughout history, doctors have known that the body and mind are connected. They treated problems in the mind by healing the body's organs. Their treatment of physical sickness showed their belief in this link, too. One way they cured physical illness was to help a patient resolve his mental or emotional difficulties. We know that mental illness is sometimes caused by a malfunction of the body's organs. Organs can fail to work properly because of poor nutrition or toxins to which we are exposed. Sometimes even medicines and vaccines harm the body.

Classical medicine has found many connections between the body and the mind. Specific organs govern different mental and emotional processes. For example:

- The kidneys control emotions of fear and anxiety.
- The lungs relate to feelings of sorrow and loss.
- The spleen governs our feelings of worry and obsession.
- The liver relates to feelings of anger, jealousy, irritation, and depression.
- The heart is at our "center," the core of our individuality and relationships. It integrates the functioning of all our other organs.

We can relieve emotional problems by treating the organs. For example, acupuncture can cure anxiety if it is focused on the kidneys. We can also strengthen the kidneys using herbs or homeopathy. This, too, will lower a person's anxiety.

Our mental health depends on many things, such as the proper health of our organs. And our organs depend on our environment to work well. Surroundings that are peaceful aid our physical health. Also, a good spiritual foundation gives us a feeling of security and well being. We can all benefit from inspiration and hopefulness in our daily lives.

Intuition influences our lives strongly. Studies show that the heart perceives first. What the heart intuits today, the brain will understand tomorrow.

Stress factors and children

The most formative time in our lives is from birth through puberty. During this period, we form our basic responses to life. So it is important to identify factors that affect our children's growth. One area to watch is the mental and emotional influences that affect a child. Another area consists of spiritual influences. A third area to pay attention to is a child's physical environment. Throughout the book are examples of the influence in the lives of intuitive children, especially in times of stress. When the mind can't think, we rely on intuition. When the body is tired, we rely on our inner voice and wisdom to provide guidance about food, exercise, and treatment.

Environment

One way to safeguard our children's environment is to ensure that they have proper nutrition, which we cover in more depth later in this book. Another way is to become aware of unhealthful toxins in the home and eliminating them. When children are sick, we can try natural remedies. We can change our old habit of reaching for prescription medicines first.

Mind and emotions

In safeguarding emotional growth in children, we can respect the role of play. When children play, they use fantasy and creativity. They imagine and act out the roles they will grow into as adults. The word *imagination* means we create the "image" of what we are to become. So play helps children grow as healthy individuals, and you'll learn how it is a keen marker for the creative-intuitive child.

Children need unstructured time for imaginative play. Today, our children often spend their time in structured activities at school. They take part in classes the teacher has planned. After school, they may play on a team in organized sports. Unstructured playtime is taken up when they passively watch television.

Children need free time. They need time in which they are not guided in a planned activity. They need free time so they can mature and develop their own unique modes of expression. And they need to develop their own understanding of the world and of other people. Children learn a lot when educators and parents guide their activities. But they also need to learn from playing on their own without the values and ideas of adults to direct them. When they play on their own, children will discover who they are in an intimate, personal way. Play also empowers them to be curious and learn to negotiate their environments safely.

Spiritual development

The third area to consider is the spiritual aspect of life. People think of having three aspects: soul, body, and spirit. The activities of the soul are emotions, thought, and creativity. The body contains physical counterparts of the soul as tissues, organs, and metabolism. The spirit is considered sacred by most cultures and religions around the world as the life-sustaining energy field permeating all. It is as much a part of us as our blood, flesh, and feelings.

Our spirits contain the heart's simple needs. The spirit holds the desires and aspirations we feel for ourselves, family, friends, and even our careers. Our needs are uncomplicated, and when they are met, we feel fulfilled and satisfied. Where does the influence of intuition enter the picture?

Intuitive intelligence permeates all aspects of the energy. Chinese philosophy and medicine emphasize the heart's importance as an organ of perception. We intuitively know from the heart, which accumulates the largest energy charge and distributes the energy to every cell, passing along information.

We want unconditional love from someone. We also want to feel that our unique ways of looking at the world have value. If we make mistakes, we need to be affirmed and forgiven despite them. We need to feel worthy of acceptance without having to prove anything to anybody. These needs are especially strong when we feel overwhelmed and powerless. We want these things and so do our children.

Children need a healthful environment. They need to be able to express creatively. They need a parent or caregiver who understands their spirit. If these factors are present, a child can deal with the stresses of living. A child can develop the qualities to lead a successful and happy life.

Our own spirituality has a greater effect on our children than material goods we may give them. It will support the developing spirits of our children. A child's spirit forms the basis of his or her emotional responses and sense of health and well being.

When children feel safe, and their physical and emotional needs are met, their intuitive and spiritual intelligences rise to the surface for development and enrichment.

Breathing space produces calm

How often have you heard, "I'm bored and there's nothing to do." You may have replied, "Go outside and play. Go watch television. Find something to do."

Next time you hear the boredom complaint, say, "Great, wonderful. Take some space." Enjoying "space" is one of the best ways for children to allow their minds and bodies to settle down and find peace. We encourage our children to relax, contemplate, or empty their minds. We may call it "take a breather," "peace and quiet," "doing nothing," "calm break," or simply being.

We use the term "space" to describe a state that is empty of expectations, conditions, and outcomes. Space connects to intuition. When we take space, or time out, we participate in unstructured time. Children and adults often experience difficulty doing this. Adults are used to the demands of performing a job. Children are accustomed to doing homework where the rules of how to use time are spelled out.

Learning to use unstructured time creatively is beneficial. If we learn to do this, we can discover our inner beauty and worthiness. Our children can, too. Do your children know how to do nothing? Can they uncover the revelation hidden in moments of stillness and silence?

We need to show our children how to use space if they are ever to gain a feeling of wholeness and inner peace. Space allows intuition to surface and be active, and children to be aware of this. They need a time to feel in control— a time when they are not being stimulated by anything outside themselves. When children listen quietly to what is inside them, they may think of music and poetry. Creating new things will teach them confidence.

We often forget that life is a process in which we are constantly creating things. We form our cells and tissues out of the energies found in the chemistry of the plant, animal, and mineral kingdoms. We create thoughts, words, and ideas from our experiences. We perceive life through the creative action of our senses and the ceaseless searching of our hearts. Children need time and space so they can explore their own abilities to be creative.

Children become aware of their power to create the way they see life by being quiet in unstructured time. Their creativity unfolds slowly and continues to show itself in the time when they are doing nothing. They miss out on this experience when they are trying to carry out predetermined goals. We do well to nurture creativity in our children. It comes to them naturally. Creativity is also the aspect that we can preserve and encourage for ourselves.

Putting the pieces together

The different types of energy have unique qualities, so they affect the body and mind differently. For example, emotional energy is irregular. When our goal is to manage this energy, we can change our activities and do things that build up the opposite physical qualities. Later chapters in the book provide strategies for managing irregular emotional energy. We can fit our actions into a regular schedule. When we behave in patterns, it lowers our emotional stress.

Children perform best when they have regular schedules or understand expectations. Specific times for meals, bedtime, playtime, homework, and family chores can ease stress they might feel. These activities create a secure framework for a child if they are done each day.

Activities that are performed at irregular times can be stressful. For example, how stressed do you feel when your activities pile up? How distressed are you when you are forced to concentrate on more than one thing at a time to get them all done? You create stress in your life when you simultaneously have to buy groceries, walk the dog, watch the children, and catch up on your work. Brain research shows that multi-tasking fatigues the brain. You create a chronic stress pattern if you repeat this kind of overload often enough. We can perform all the needed tasks by putting our activities on a regular schedule. We also gain the time to focus on the attention to detail that they need. We manage our time to regulate our emotional energy.

Stress disperses and fragments an individual's energy. Sometimes children read an assignment while they are watching TV. They may try to go over their math while listening to distracting music. These activities generate stress. Parents might try providing "space" around homework activities. Children then are free from interruptions that interfere with their focus of attention. They can do their homework in peace and quiet.

The things we have been discussing are so obvious that we often overlook them. We do not credit them with the impact they have on our lives. We look at the activity rather than energy that it is producing and how it affects the body and mind. The body and mind operate on energies. Every activity produces some form of energy ripple.

Our health is best when our activities radiate creative and non-stressful energies. These energies contribute to our growing sense of wholeness. They are the meaning of *heilida*, health—the oneness and sacredness of life.

Be practical: health mindfulness

- Understand that health is your natural state, and you participate creatively in it by your choices.

- Honor the signals from your mind and body about how to create balance in your life. If you do experience stress or disease, it is only part of the natural process of learning balance.

- Integrate and digest everything you take in. Don't overwhelm yourself or your children with food, addictions, thoughts, sensory stimuli, and the like. The key to healthy metabolism is in balance.

- Be thoughtful about the *basics* of health. Eat proper food. Maintain a nontoxic physical environment. Take care of your health processes that strengthen etheric energy and support your physical health.

- Find your own spiritual perspective. Share your thoughts about the "big" questions in life with your child. Give them a means of embracing their experience. You promote your health for the mental, emotional, and etheric energies and their relationship to one another.

- Now that you understand the basic structures of the mind and body and the interface of etheric energy, let's move to the topic of intuitive intelligence.

Chapter Review

- Energy creates matter, and matter produces and changes into energy.
- All natural functions of the mind and body produce energy and respond to it.
- Mental energy mirrors our spiritual feelings. Our spiritual outlook helps us understand our role in life.

- Emotional energy affects our thinking and our emotional responses to things we experience.

- Etheric energy helps the body function physically.

- Stress is connected to emotional energy. Emotional energy flies out in all directions. It comes from our thoughts and our activities. It is dispersed and fragmented. Its nature is uneven and it produces inconsistent effects. Activities that are like this will create emotional energy. They could cause problems that stem from inconsistency and lack of order.

- Stress stimulates us because it is so demanding. The over-stimulation tires us. Then our feelings become depressed and our energy level goes down. We can change this and program thoughts and activities that produce order and structure, leading to happiness and well being.

2

Children With Intuitive Intelligence

Intuition is what your brain knows how to do when you leave it alone.
—Dr. Paul MacLean, former Chief of Brain
Evolution, National Institute of Mental Health, 1988

Intuition is a natural intelligence that all children possess. Intuitive development depends on the environment, parental support, and education. Some children are highly skilled or gifted in this talent in the same way that others have a talent for math, music, languages, or physical dexterity. This chapter discusses how children with intuitive intelligence experience their worlds and interact with their environments. We maintain that intuitive intelligence is the single intelligence that enables a person to know their wholeness, to be aware, and manage their personal energy.

Intuition became valid to mainstream thought after Carl Jung, a Swiss psychiatrist, suggested that people had different ways of learning or absorbing information. Jung included intuition as one of the four ways we process information. They are:

1. Thinking.
2. Feeling.
3. Sensing.
4. Intuition.

Jung said that the human brain has four different areas that go with the four processing modes, and each of us uses all four areas of our brain. Jung's simple premise has grown into modern-day neuroscience, mapping brain functions and providing evidence of how people process intuitive information. (See Appendix for further information.)

Each of us has a preference in how we view and relate to the world. This book provides information on how children with an intuitive learning style and intuitive intelligence view and interact with people, tasks, and the environment.

Intuitive intelligence

Intuition was perceived as the psychic woo-woo of spiritualists 50 years ago. Today it has been deservedly recognized as a valid human intelligence along with others:

- Physical intelligence.
- Mental-creative intelligence.
- Emotional-social intelligence.
- Intuitive intelligence.
- Spiritual intelligence.

Intuitive intelligence stands as an entity deserving recognition. Brain mapping using EEG topography found that creativity and intuition are associated with theta waves usually linked with daydreaming or fantasizing. Theta waves are calm states in which intellectual activity at the conscious level isn't occurring. Children and adults diagnosed with ADHD produce excessive theta waves.

Intuitive intelligence operates on gestalts or whole pieces of information and functions from our memory, not logic. Intuitive ability is finally recognized as the fuel behind innovation, creative thinking, inspiration, and psychic experiences.

Let's clarify terms:

Intuitive intelligence—a system of processing information from a gestalt that arrives spontaneously, beyond intellectually known information, or evident thought. Every human has an intuitive processing system. Like any intelligence, different people will have varying degrees of strength.

Intuition—a talent or ability to grasp or understand spontaneous perception, feeling, or information. This talent would be a strength of the intuitive intelligence range.

We are discussing children whose intuitive intelligence manifests in different ways along a continuum of normal skills to gifted talents:

- Children who *learn through feelings* and process information *kinesthetically*. (Intuitive learning mode.)
- Children who are creative and artistic and *intuition drives their motivation*. (Artistic drive for exploring and creating.)
- Children whose intuitive intelligence is *like a radar reading other people* and understanding them. (Empathy and interpersonal skills.)
- Children who have *intuitive episodes* like dreams or a flash of creative insight. (Deep insight, precognition.)
- Children who are *psychic*. (Awareness of non-physical worlds through all senses or a specific sense.)

Intuition is the common denominator of these talents and all children have the same intuitive capacities. Similar to musical prodigies and math geniuses, children display their talents differently.

Intuitive children with highly tuned sensory perceptions display their gifts in what our cultures might think are unconventional ways. For example, how many parents are ready to believe that their children see ghosts or who, at a young age, have an entrepreneurial idea that could be successful?

Education, parenting, and psychology professionals recognize that children have multiple intelligences, and intuitive intelligence is the new kid on the block. All intelligences exist on a continuum of normal to gifted. There are math prodigies, musical geniuses, and intuitive psychics. The traits for intuitive intelligence cluster into several groups:

- Creative and inspired artists.
- Sensitive and empathic feelers.
- Talents involving inner psychic awareness.
- Spiritual intuitives.

Creative, inspired artist

John always remembers hearing music in his head. This music playing was his "normal." He constantly hummed, which irritated his teachers and classmates. From the time John was 7 years old, he experienced interruptions in his musical pursuits. His parents divorced when he was 7 years old. At age 8, he pulled his drowning younger sister from the pool in his backyard. How she went over the fence surrounding the pool was never uncovered. At age 9, he developed food allergies, which left his mind fuzzy, schoolwork difficult, and his body fatigued. Yet, John's intuition continued to be curious about this music. In his tough times, he turned to his creativity.

He learned to read music. His mother taught him the basics of the piano, and then John went on to learn the guitar. By age 11, he was playing the music he heard in his head when he wasn't in school. Music absorbed his attention and poured from his soul. When others worried about his social skills and his lack of other interests, he stuck to his creativity. As a college graduate, John took menial jobs and played in a band until he was discovered and offered a recording contract. He is now an internationally known musician.

Empathic feeler

Eleven-year-old Laurie was sprawled across her bed and crying silently. She had just finished reading the book *The Yearling* by Marjorie Kinnan Rawlings. The story portrayed the life of a boy named Jody Baxter, a solitary soul who developed a friendship with a deer. Her dad sat on the corner of her bed, ready to listen. Laurie discussed her sadness from the book, which reminded her of a classmate who was sad because his brother, a Marine, had died recently in the Middle East. Then there was her best friend whose parents were getting a divorce.

"I feel it all here, Dad." Laurie pressed her heart like she was holding her emotions inside. One drop of sadness turned into a steady stream of tears that formed a puddle. Such are moments in the world of empathic children.

Spiritual psychic

Life is a flame that is always burning itself out, but it catches fire again every time a child is born.

—George Bernard Shaw

Maria's story tells how her spiritual gift gave her a sense of trust during her grandfather's death.

Maria thoroughly enjoyed spending summers with her grandparents at their ranch. Her grandfather taught her all about horses, and she was an accomplished rider at age 11 when she visited during a hot summer season in dry West Texas.

Maria first noticed that her grandfather's skin was dotted with crusty open sores around his throat and chin. When she asked what happened, she noticed that his eyes turned downward as he said that he cut himself shaving. All of her grandfather's signals said he wasn't telling her the truth. Something else was going on and she was curious.

At dinner, she gazed across the table at him when he wasn't looking. As was her habit when watching people's energy, she let her perception soften, and she noticed a tall, whitish figure behind her grandfather. She knew this was an angel, and she figured her grandfather would die soon. Whenever she saw angels around people, it was to help them die; at least this had been true for Maria, based on her personal experiences.

Maria was a brave, young woman that summer, as she never asked her grandfather about the sores on his neck again. She heard the family whispers about how painful lung cancer was. When school started, Maria chose to stay at the ranch, sitting next to her grandfather's bed, and watching and waiting with his angels. When her grandfather died, Maria was sad, but didn't feel such a painful loss as other family members, as she could see him with the angels.

Maria showed the intuitive traits of deeper understanding of a bigger picture and clairvoyance or ability to see into the nonphysical. She felt the love and compassion from this reflection.

An Intuitive Continuum

This book clarifies that intuitive intelligence, similar to other intelligences, is a continuum of skills. Skills range from an ability to feel a friend's downer energy to the heightened intuitive, who displays a psychic ability, such as clairvoyance. A child who takes music lessons and has a good ear for music is far different from a musical prodigy even though both demonstrate musical intelligence. A smart high schooler, who does algebraic equations in his head, has mathematical intelligence, the same as a 15-year-old who ponders quantum physics as a freshman at MIT. They exist on the same intelligence continuum, but show different aptitudes.

The confusion around intuition being a valid intelligence persisted because of how different groups use the words like intuition, psychic, and spiritual gifts synonymously. The origin of the word *intuition* from Middle English denotes spiritual insight or spiritual communication and may evoke images of ghostly séances. The term *psyche* means "of the soul," so psychic refers to people being in touch with the non-physical, what we think of as the spiritual world. People still confuse the terms today, and so we suggest using the inclusive phrase, "intuitive intelligence." Our support for children's talents has to provide them a resilient foundation against those who don't understand. Tara's story provides an example of how an intuitive person is viewed by her peers.

As an intuitive high school student, Tara Paterson always felt different from the other kids she went to school with. She was disappointed when she sensed a student being fake or inauthentic. She had an uncanny way of knowing when other students were gossiping or being cruel to her or others. Tara quickly learned she wasn't able to conform to one of the "cliques," which left her feeling like an outcast. She became an easy target for being picked on because she didn't have the ability to change her personality. High school was an emotionally challenging time for Tara's intuitive style.

Tara recalls when her girlfriends were cruel to her. She also remembered being the target of a Halloween prank during her junior year of high school when several girls decided it would be funny to egg her in the face at point-blank range. What hurt most was that the one she thought was her best friend was part of the cruelty. Is this what having friends was like?

Such incidences of bullying are common for intuitive and sensitive children and teens, even adults. We can only be authentic and true to our nature, and cruelty is learned. John the musician was teased in high school because of his artistic nature. When he won awards at the state level for his thespian activities, his peers could also applaud his victory, but as John says, "My proving myself was a long fight to get the approval of other kids I'd probably never see again."

Stand steadfast to support intuitive intelligence

Our point here is that our kids need our support and you, the parent, are the only one who knows how to interpret your intuitive experiences or those of your children. As a parent, do you believe your child is a deep feeler, sees ghosts or angels, or uses internal interpretation to make sense of his or her world? If so, then here are some questions for your consideration:

1. Are you able to suspend judgment and accept the experience as your child reports it?
2. Can you be a responsive listener?
3. If you need more information, will you educate yourself through books or other avenues of information?
4. If you need help, will you ask for it without embarrassment of your child's gift?
5. If medical doctors suggest medications for which your child may be too sensitive, will you seek alternative explanations also?
6. Will you accept intuitive intelligence as a normal way to learn, develop skills, and interpret life's opportunities and challenges?
7. Will you celebrate your child's talents and diversity?

Who can decide if psychic ability is the mortal mind reaching its potential? Or is psychic manifestation simply our humanness touching our mysticism? Is an intuitive scientist like Einstein a creative genius, a mystic, or an intuitive with great insight?

Those you ask will have different opinions about intuition or psychic abilities. Some opinions are supportive; others will consider intuition as non-reliable. The authors have witnessed the courts in Oklahoma take away custody of a young mother's two children because she was honest with the court when she said she earned her living as a psychic. In the meantime, *Newsweek* magazine tells the story of Laura Day, a corporate intuitive who "has become a hot commodity" as the psychic business consultant. Laura Day, the author of three books, the first of which is *Practical Intuition,* tells how all persons can develop their intuitive intelligence.

Parents' intuition opens with child's birth

Some parents' intuitive abilities start with a connection to their children. Caron knew her child was a girl before the doctor even confirmed she was pregnant. She had consistent dreams about how her daughter would look and what her temperament would be as an adult. Caron's client, Marilyn, experienced an unusual introduction to her daughter.

No one in her family would believe Marilyn's psychic experience at 2 a.m. except her husband, who had grown used to her visions and the reality they showed. Sometimes Marilyn herself needed a reality check, and the morning after the "vision," she called her spiritual coach, Dr. Caron Goode.

"Caron, I had a weird experience last night, and wanted to get your feedback on it."

"Hey, Marilyn, good to hear from you. What happened last night?"

"I woke up at 2 a.m. because someone was calling my name, but I heard it in my head, not with my physical ears. I sat up, wide awake, and in front of me, at the foot of the bed, was a soft light. If its presence hadn't lingered there a while, I would question whether it was there at all."

"Marilyn, what was your feeling associated with the light?"

"I felt pure love, wasn't frightened, but what the light said was disturbing."

"And that was…."

"Well, this is weird, Caron."

"All our conversations are weird, that's why we love sharing."

"Okay…okay. The light said that her soul wants to be born through me, live with my family, so she can do her work in the world."

"The light specified that she would be female?"

"Yes. And when I told James this morning, he seemed okay with it. But you remember James and I agreed no more children after the first two.

"I am surprised and pleased that James took it so casually."

"Yes, he seemed intrigued that the soul would choose us as parents, to have one appear and request it is…well…"

"I know, weird. So how can I help?"

"James and I would like to talk this through with you. Can we make an appointment?"

James and Marilyn didn't need the appointment the next morning because the soul of the soft white light woke them that night and signaled its readiness to be born. The effect of the early morning lovemaking produced a daughter, Megan, nine months later.

Even though Marilyn had always accepted her visionary capacity and high intuition, she was curious to see how Megan would mature in intuitive abilities. Megan had great empathy, as she cried with other toddlers whose tears moved her. Even as Megan played with her brother and sister, she was independent in her behavior, and didn't depend on them for her entertainment, as the third child in a household might.

One behavior that Marilyn and James noticed about their daughter was her sensitivity to their moods. Another was her sensitivity to the moods of family members. If James came home from the office in a cranky mood, Megan would engage him in a game of peek-a-boo or hugs. Because Marilyn was a stay-at-home-mom, Megan was more used to her mom's ups and downs, and still seemed to feel them with her.

Marilyn and Megan showed intuition in their sensitivity to other's feelings, desired to cheer others up, had deep empathy, and trusted their vision.

Intuitives interactions with the world

For reference, we can say that an intuitive has a certain predisposition or temperament to processing information through

- sensation or feeling.
- flashes of perception.
- knowing.
- creative emotion.
- visceral or gut level feelings.
- psychic gifts.

Do any of these traits of an intuitive sound like you or your child?

If you are an intuitive, you may find yourself drawn to work with people because you influence others well and find personal satisfaction in selling, serving, training, inspiring, counseling, coaching, or teaching.

You are compassionate, creative, and convincing. Your enthusiasm could spill over in conversation as loudness, restlessness, or impulsiveness unless you monitor or regulate your energy. You enjoy people, good times, and group activities. Your intuitive children do also.

You feel deeply about people or causes. You have to monitor your own emotional flow so as not to imbibe of others' emotions or affect them.

These traits are a composite of the intuitive-type temperament, and we find that intuitives have differing levels of sensitivity influenced and changed by the other factors. These include biological aspects, self-worth levels, environments, social teachers, and stressors and traumas.

So think of the intuitive temperament as the unchanging 20 percent of our personalities that serves as our steady anchor. The other five factors that shape our personality will influence the 80 percent of who we become and how we develop. An intuitive parent will want to watch their children's development to monitor sensitivity and influence the situation to insure successful results. The following scales are areas to observe as your child matures.

How does an intuitive relate to people?

Quiet..Talkative

Less Sensitive....................................More Sensitive

Loner...............Small Groups...........Loves a Crowd

How does an intuitive relate to tasks?

Laissez Faire...................................…..Doer

Procrastinates...............................…...Finishes

Distracted...................................…Focused

How does an intuitive relate to the environment?

Less Sensitive...................................More Sensitive

Initiates\Controls Environment..............Reacts to Environment

How does an intuitive relate to stress?

Escape.......................Freeze.....................Face it

---

Intuitive traits

Around 75,000,000 intuitives, about a fourth of the United States population, may display the following personality characteristics:

- *Shyness.*
- *Fearfulness.*
- *Low-sensory threshold.*
- *Sensitivity to energies in their environment.*
- *Sensitivity to people's moods and energies.*
- *Reflective.*
- *Empathic.*
- *Intelligent.*
- *Creative.*
- *Aware.*
- *Conscientious.*

Their traits comprise a style of interaction with people and environments that can result in intuitives feeling like a round peg in a square hole. Exactly! Providing a person with a perception more expansive than that of the linear mind, these round-peg traits are now valued. The right kind of nurturing and training empowers intuitives to lead exceptional lives of contributions and service.

As authors and speakers, we are delighted when someone says to us, "I'm an intuitive, and I didn't even know it. I just thought I was weird and made it okay." Tara had similar thoughts and feelings the first time she discovered her intuitive style and its fit in her world.

Tara explains, "At the age of 27, I attended a wellness seminar, where I was introduced to a technique called *kinesiology,* also known as muscle testing. The body responds kinesthetically to questions asked by the health practitioner by a gentle push on an outstretched arm. After answering several questions using this process, the seminar leader gave me my profile with the title of *Iris—The Natural Intuitive.* The information described personality qualities such as strengths or traits that undermine your health.

Tara said, "I was amazed at how accurately this piece of paper described me. For the first time I realized who I was and why I always felt so different from everyone else.

Many times people told me, 'You're altruistic, too trusting. You need to be grounded. How do you know that?' I wasn't always able to explain how I knew what I knew or why I felt the way I did, but when I read my profile I understood. It described me as being

- An idealistic humanitarian who loved helping others.
- One with a creative imagination.
- Able to intuit what is not immediately apparent to another.
- Confident in trusting my feelings.
- A natural psychic with an intuition that would never let me down.

This feedback was a turning point in my journey to trusting what I know and learning to work with my natural gifts, which brought me to becoming a parent coach for intuitive parents and children."

Chapter Review

Intuition is a natural intelligence that all children have the capacity to develop. Some children are more highly skilled or gifted in this intelligence.

Intuitive intelligence takes its place in the sphere of natural human intelligences.

- Physical intelligence.
- Mental-creative intelligence.
- Emotional-social intelligence.
- Intuitive intelligence.
- Spiritual intelligence.

The traits for intuitive intelligence cluster into several groups: creative and inspired artists, sensitive and empathic feelers, and talents involving inner psychic awareness and spiritual gifts.

Children with an intuitive temperament respond to life in predictable ways, and their ability to relate to people, tasks, their environments, and to stressors influence how they express their intuition.

Knowing the challenges faced by the intuitive child enables parents to discuss, plan, and help with personality and skill development. Children can also have intuitive episodes, which make them aware of and in communication with the non-physical world.

3

The Intuitive Learner

Cease trying to work everything out with your minds. It will get you no-where. Live by intuition and inspiration and let your whole life be Revelation.

—Eileen Caddy

The Intuitive Learner

"The intuitive learner likes to experience life. Forget about watching a video or reading a book—intuitive children learn by experience. They use their bodies to receive feedback from their environment by means of sensory organs in their muscles and joints. They have an excellent sense of their bodies in space and movement reigns when it comes to their talent. The intuitive learner has to get out there and engage," explains Ken Keis.

An international expert on personal styles, leadership, and parenting, Ken Keis is president and CEO of Consulting Resource Group International, Inc., founded in 1979 (*www.crgleader.com*). Professionals herald CRG as one of the top global resource centers for personal and professional development. Ken's purpose is to help others discover and live their purpose. Because our mission is bringing intuitive intelligence out of the closet, we interviewed Ken about intuitive learners. Ken's son is an intuitive learner, and he shares his parenting stories.

Ken continues: "Sometimes intuitive children are in an environment where compliance is required, like sitting in a desk all day at school, or rules which pronounce 'don't do this, don't do that.' Intuitive children find this environment difficult. Their whole essence of who they are wants to engage in what's going on and what's happening.

"Then all of a sudden, these kids are misbehaving. In essence, they need to disperse their personal energy rather than stay bundled up. Compliance isn't part of their nuance. These kids need to have an outlet for pent-up energy and still follow standards for behavior.

"There are some new initiatives in education to restore movement and physical activity in educational settings on a daily basis. These specific children are able to engage learning because they need this adrenalin component as part of their learning practice. Now educators are starting to catch on that education is not about sitting in a desk without moving for six hours. Instead kids are sitting and bouncing on round exercise balls or doing micro exercises for 10 to 20 minutes in the morning. As a result, learning has increased because intuitive children can physically engage the environment."

Intuition, emotions, and thoughts

On the other side of the coin, intuitive learners engage emotions and thoughts differently than other modes of learning. Some have great insights about what's going on with other people emotionally. Adults discount children's intuitive nature, thinking they do not have insight. That's where the child's spirit gets crushed and their personhood is discounted inappropriately. Instead of them feeling appreciated, their self-worth goes down or they move into a peer group where they feel appreciated.

An adult might say, "you couldn't know that yet because you're only 12." Well, who says that they couldn't know that yet? Are we paying attention to the fact that these kids' talents are ignored? Or are we wondering why they're frustrated? Maybe children with intuitive styles are not doing well because we haven't embraced their gifts and talents.

My purpose is to make sure that others live their purpose and that includes the intuitive learner. A lot of times, kids are not given permission to exceed, excel, or have gifts and talents that are contrary to the norm. For example, my family and I were at a Christmas party. My aunt was making some comments to my son, who is gifted in music. He can sit down, listen to a tune, and play it. The melody rolls out of his fingers. I have no idea how he does it, but he has that gift. My aunt said to my son, "What are you going to do? I know that music is important to you, but what are you going to do for a real job because you'll never make any money in music?"

Part of the need of the intuitive style is that routines and structure around compliance can contribute as much stress as conflict. Frustration comes from *the demand* for compliance. I'll give you an example we had five years ago from my son's music teacher who was traditional in her teaching approach.

Tim needs to learn the structure of music so that he can be a great player later on if he so desires. However, the instructor was this pragmatic, linear teacher. Tim, kind of being off the wall, in the moment, just plays from his heart. The situation was not working because the environment was completely stressful for him, and also stressful for the teacher, because she wasn't able to connect with him.

Then, enter the new keyboard instructor who noticed that Tim was not paying attention during the lessons for his piano. He said, "Tim, what's the most distracting thing you can think of right now and how outlandish is it?" He gave him permission to have one minute of completely off-the-wall thought. He said, "Tim, is that done now? Now can we focus on this?" The moment was brilliant!

The instructor said to himself, "I can't stop this, but what I'm going to do is work with it, to release this distraction or this idea that's going on in his head." Rather than being frustrated or upset as an adult or teacher, Tim can have his moment, and then they resume the music. A highly respectful and incredible relationship developed. The instructor did not let him get away with anything and held him to being compliant as far as standards and practice. The instructor worked with 11-year-old Tim and not against him.

Rather than trying to change Tim, the instructor achieved the outcome. If we went back five years and kept my son on that first teacher track, he would have quit music a long time ago. Our parenting style and the new instructor's teaching style was to appeal to Tim's experiential, intuitive nature.

Are intuitive kids entrepreneurial?

There are young entrepreneurs, ages 10 to 13, who have this intuitive nature toward some kind of business opportunity. Mom and Dad, who come from different environments, don't understand their children's interest. Most schools do not appeal to the entrepreneur. Consulting Resource Group's research on the entrepreneurial assessment shows that as a younger child, entrepreneurs had a lemonade stand, a paper route, or a babysitting service. As a kid, they ran a little business, which they creatively developed without fear, just curiosity and inspiration.

Are parents supporting that entrepreneurial curiosity? Do kids have an outlet for their desire to explore or experiment? Are parents embracing children's interests in arts, drama, writing, or growing flowers?

Successful business people like Michael Dell and Bill Gates dropped out of college. They didn't fit the left-brain educational model. Rather their interest was to experience what made them curious, and explore what intrigued their minds. Some of us are wired to experience life by engaging, exploring, and creating.

Specialty schools for fine arts have become the norm in certain school districts. They serve the kids who have a gift in drama, music, or the arts, and use the whole brain approach to creativity and intuitive capacity. The traditional or standard school system isn't allowing them to explore those skills. Right now, nontraditional venues for intuitive children have never been higher. How do we embrace those interests and make sure that we are playing to their gifts, talents, interests, and abilities as soon as we can identify them?

Ken Keis reminds us that our intuitive children's personal styles and learning environments require a response to the context of their learning. We cannot expect them to respond to the way we want them to be. These children demand that we be responsive to who they are.

Tara as an entrepreneur

Coauthor Tara Paterson's entrepreneurial discovery as a young child was the common practice of a roadside lemonade stand. However her entrepreneurial spirit revealed itself as a college student and in her early years as a wife and mother.

Tara shares her story:

I worked at night as a bartender and a server while my husband worked during the day so one of us was always home with our son. I read one of Suzie Orman's books and was inspired because her first job was as a server, and she gave credit to the job for being entrepreneurial. For me it definitely was. I could not have imagined working a full-time job, confined to an office all day, away from my son, Adam.

While bartending one afternoon, the vice president of a real estate company was dining in my section. Before he left, he handed me his card and asked if I would consider interviewing for a job with their company. I was flattered and thought it would be a nice change, so I decided to give it a shot. I was hired on the spot and found a mom who was at home with her son to watch mine. I felt grown up, at first.

Within a short time, I felt trapped by the confines of a full-time job. Before I had a flexible schedule and was home during the day with Adam. Then our schedule changed to getting up early, getting us ready for the day, and making it to work on time. Adam and I returned home in time for dinner and his early bedtime.

By the weekend, I was exhausted and had to do all of my chores and errands. It was complete drudgery. To make matters worse, I hated the position at the new company and desperately wanted to be moved to a spot that matched my personality and style. They refused because they believed they knew how to best use my strengths, only they miscalculated the strength of my self-confidence and competence.

Before too long, I went to the bathroom in the office to cry out my regret at my choice. My intuition was screaming at me to leave. My mind echoed back about making it work and being in the system to be successful. I longed to be back at home with my son, and within a few short months, I quit.

I enjoyed the freedom and flexibility of working in a restaurant. I had the joy of being home all day with Adam and more time to myself. I haven't worked a full-time job for any one else since.

This is far from the end of Tara's entrepreneurial journey as she went on to create several businesses from home: a national awards program, a certified coach, which coincidentally, was the position Tara desperately wanted to have in the real estate company—a coach for real estate agents.

In the face of much adversity, Tara has remained true to her inner passion and has learned to trust her intuition to guide her toward the work she is doing today—an author and certified coach for parents. Tara's intuition never stopped guiding her toward her goals. She also follows in the footsteps of people such as Bill Gates and Michael Dell, as she never completed her college degree either.

The message here is strong: trusting one's intuition is the road map to a life of mastery. Are intuitive people entrepreneurial? Perhaps it's one of their greatest assets—to dance to their own beat and empower others to join in the dance.

Environment, people, and tasks

Everyone deals with these three aspects of their lives according to our temperament and preferences. Explore these aspects in regard to your intuitive child.

1. We negotiate our **environment**, whether it's the geographic area we live in, our home milieu, the classroom setting, work conditions, or emotional atmospheres.

2.   Some persons enjoy other **people**, love networking, conversing, playing, helping, influencing, and mentoring.

3. Finally, some persons enjoy **tasks** more than they enjoy people. Examples include those who love to tinker on cars or fix machines; computer lovers who enjoy researching, writing, designing Websites, creating codes, and gaming; truckers who like their solitary long rides; and artists and builders who work with their hands in mediums that allow creativity.

To help you discover how your specific child relates to these three variables, assess your child's responses to environment, people, and tasks on the following scales. The new information gained from direct observation helps you in shaping your child's environment and understanding his or her motivations.

Dealing with people

An intuitive child who loves being around people can easily make new friends and fits in well with the group. This is a strength of the talkative one. The child who is quieter tends to observe people, watching actions and reactions, sometimes reading energy of feelings and emotions. If your child's tendency is to the quiet end, then the daydreamer with creative, artistic talent may be churning through ideas. The focus could be on their inner world. This is the loner or a child who tolerates small groups and may enjoy the family pet or nature walks better than other playmates. They are less resilient in handling empathy.

The more talkative child leans toward influencing others or being too easily influenced by others. The more talkative and crowd-oriented intuitives tends to be less sensitive in their feelings and are resilient in dealing with people. Their confidence tends to be stronger than a more sensitive child, who may feel unsure of themselves around people. They may not like the way certain feelings of specific people affect their own bubble of energy. We've witnessed toddlers who said another person's energy "hurt" them. We've listened to sensitive teens describe how they choose to attend one party but not another based upon the emotional atmosphere of the place. Some parties are toxic; other parties are fun!

The following assessment provides a graph as to where you see your intuitive child. Mark an × along the continuums.

How does an intuitive relate to people?

Quiet..Talkative

More Sensitive...Less Sensitive

Loner....................Small Groups..................Loves a Crowd

Dealing with tasks

Observing how your child deals with tasks ranges from procrastination to loving the work and finishing. One difficulty with creative intuitives is how deeply they get into the task at hand. For example, 8-year-old Chloe developed a fascination with rocks and crystals, which lasted for three months.

She read books, cracked rocks open, collected rocks from around her home, and built a rock garden. She forgot to come in for dinner and argued that she needed to read before bedtime. Then her curiosity suddenly disappeared, and her normal, mindful behavior returned. Does your child explore so deeply that he loses track of time? Does she become so involved that her effort goes beyond what is necessary? We have found that pushing creative children into a task that doesn't interest them breeds procrastination and distraction. Can it be okay that a loner, sensitive child spends the summer reading Nancy Drew mysteries instead of out playing with other kids? Is it all right if your child skips dinner because he is still on the Internet exploring how dolphins communicate?

The following assessment provides a graph as to how you see your intuitive child's approach to tasks. Please mark an × along the continuums.

How does an intuitive relate to tasks?

Laissez Faire...Doer
Procrastinates..Finishes
Distracted ....Focused

Chapter Review

In this chapter Ken Keis discussed that intuitive children learn through engaging life actively. Schools, which support physical education, interactive learning environments, and the expressive arts, suit children with intuitive learning styles better than traditional schools. Creative intuitives are interested entrepreneurs even in childhood.

Parents can find clues as to how their children interact with people, tasks, and the environment by noting where their children's behaviors fall on the appropriate continuum of behaviors. Then we can see their strengths and guide intuitives to acquire the skills they need for success.

4

Negotiating Environments

The intellect has little to do on the road to discovery. There comes a leap in consciousness, call it intuition or what you will, and the solution comes to you and you don't know how or why.

—Albert Einstein

Observing negotiations

An intuitive child moves through different environments every day, and each environment presents opportunities and challenges for learning new skills. How a child handles those opportunities or challenges is called negotiating, which has varied interpretations: getting around, moving through, clearing the way, or coping with.

With an intuitive child, we are working with three levels of the environment:

- The physical world.
- The non-physical world.
- The spiritual world.

Calvin's Mom explored preschools as well as daycare options for her 2-year-old when she had to return to full time work. Mom is an intuitive parent whose eyes welled up with tears when she walked through a comfortable, cozy school that accepted preschoolers at age 3. Rather than run all over town looking at dozens of preschools, she trusted her intuition and saved herself a lot of wasted time. She knew this was her son's preschool when he turned 3 years old, but that was a year away.

In the meantime, her friend, a Navy wife, decided she would love to watch Calvin to help her 1-year-old daughter socialize. Observing Calvin enter the new environment, he first reviewed the toys and started exploring. Through time, he didn't get much response from the 1-year-old, but got huge rewards for playing with the cat and dog. He learned he couldn't throw balls or Frisbees around the younger child, and had to negotiate new rules. His parents prepared him for the move by visits to the new house for brief periods of time for play or nap, and then extended his day.

Calvin definitely loved people, and this helped him adjust to new environments. If a new person didn't feel right to him, he simply did not want to stay. His intuitive intelligence steered him clear of people who did not feel right to him. As long as there were toys, he played well by himself, but too much activity could overwhelm him. The self-soothing techniques he learned were to sing to himself and dance around. Observing Calvin's behaviors and adjustments to new environments enabled his parents to make the best choices in his early years for caregivers, as well as his early education.

In his nonphysical world, Calvin's mom reported that during a nighttime nursing session, he looked up at the ceiling, smiled, and then babbled for a while at whatever he saw before returning to nursing. She reported that feeling was peaceful for both of them.

Assess your intuitive child

How does your child respond to his or her environment? The following assessments provide a graph as to how you observe your child. Please mark an × along the continuums. We use the term *sensitive* on the graph to describe several factors:

1. Overwhelming versus comfortable sensory information. Loud sounds can startle children. Constant background noises cause increasing irritation over time. Soothing music or pleasant aromas such as lavender can stimulate energy and creativity. Blinking disco lights trigger emotionality and dim lights foster quiet.

2. Reactions to pollution, whether toxic chemicals or noises from people, machines, or traffic. A little leaguer in Los Angeles is more prone to asthma from environmental pollution than one who plays in Atlanta. So you can observe sensitivity in how a child responds to the environment. An older brother loves to play soccer, and the younger brother sits in the car and reads a book, complaining to Mom that he hates the yelling of the crowd.

How does an intuitive relate to the environment?

Less Sensitive..More Sensitive

Initiates/Controls Environment.........................Reacts to Environment

We have observed that children who are less sensitive are better able to initiate action, make change happen, or learn to control their environment. On the other hand, children who are more sensitive are shy of and reactive to the environment. All of us will have both responses in our lives, but we are likely to have a general pattern that parents can observe.

In this book, we encourage parents of intuitive children to be aware of your overly sensitive child's feelings to people, sounds, smells, pollutions, and lights. Sensitivities can have a biochemical basis such as allergies, hypersensitive immune system, or hypersensitive nervous system. If intuitive children are shy or don't handle change easily, then moving through change in small steps, as Calvin's mom did for him when she went back to work, greatly enhances their adaptability.

Belief that you make change happen

How an intuitive responds to the environment will determine how successfully he or she uses intuitive intelligence. Do you believe that you control what happens in your life or do you feel that your actions are controlled by outside forces like fate or God? Do you make change happen or does change happen to you? How successful intuitives are in life depends upon this very factor.

As parents we want to empower intuitive children to take charge of their lives and develop their ability to say no to ghosts, yes to inspiration and creativity, and to get back up again after falling down.

1. **Making change happen** refers to your belief or feeling that you have control over events and can influence your environment. Your motivation comes from inside you. You take action, make things happen, and move ahead. Your own actions determine your rewards.

2. **If change happens to you,** in contrast, then you feel or believe an external force such as fate, luck, or God guides your destiny. Rather than being motivated from inside, environmental factors motivate you. You may feel like what you get in life is just the way it is.

We will have both responses in our lives at different stages of development. If you parent an intuitive child, observe the tendency, so you can guide your child with encouragement, smiles, and support to take action when needed. We want our intuitive children to feel motivated from inside themselves, and they aren't just born that way. We have to help them learn the skills they need based upon what you observed and marked on the continuum chart.

Whether a child feels confident to direct his world depends upon responsive, accepting parents and whether or not their environments traumatize or impact them adversely. Children learn very early in life that their needs will be met through responsive parents. The older children learn to make appropriate choices and experience success, and they develop a belief that their actions will produce results.

Children who do not find their world positively responsive learn that their needs are not always met when they need it, but whenever their environment provides it. They tend to believe that the environment influences them, and that they don't always have control of circumstances. They are easily stressed.

The Child Who Makes Things Happen	*The Child to Whom Change Happens*
Is proactive	*Is reactive*
Is motivated to take action from inner knowing	*Waits to respond to circumstances before choosing to act*
Responds better to stress	*Stress can overwhelm*
Can manage behaviors and emotions—better self-regulation	*Better behaviors and emotions can run the child—learns through trial and error or skill building*
Prefers structure and plan	*Goes with the flow*
Prefers to own problem-solve	*Tendency to blame outside sources*
Feels guilt when fails test and resolves to study better	*Blames the test as being too hard or the teacher as being ineffective*
Not easily influenced by other's opinions	*Is easily swayed by other's opinions or emotions*
Exerts good self-control	*Makes less effort to exert self-control*
Tend to work well by themselves	*Tends to work better with direction or with a team*
Has more confidence in his or her skills and ability	*Has less confidence in his or her skills and abilities*

Natural Intelligences	Plus Intuitive Intelligence =
Physical Prowess Enhanced by Intuitive Intelligence	
Physical	*Learns by doing, has exceptional kinesthesia, motor skills, sense of timing, and movement with the body.*
Creative, Inspired Intuitive	
Mental-Creative	*Inspired, inventive, creative, follows inner music, ideas, and actions motivated by internal genius. Can daydream, be distracted, learns to focus, and learns through experimentation.*
Empathic Intuitive	
Emotional-Social	*Reads others, feels others, defines self in relation to others. Needs boundaries, emotional management skills, self-identification, and confidence.*
Psychic Intuitive	
Intuitive	*Expanded awareness of the nonphysical worlds or subtle energy fields through receptors in the biochemistry. Exhibits talents of subtle knowing, hearing, seeing, telepathy, and other talents.*
Spiritual Intuitive	
Spiritual	*Intuition serves kids with spiritual intelligence as the doorway and interpreter to connection with inner worlds.*

The good news is that all of us start at the place of dependence as infants and learn to negotiate our environments in our toddler and preschool years. As we gain confidence in negotiating our environments, we explore more. Young children take their clues from their parents and caregivers.

The ability to control, impact, or influence their environments is essential for intuitive or psychic children. For example, imagine a 3-year-old who sees a ghost that frightens her. She feels helpless to take action that gains her feelings of confidence or safety. She spends many nights in fear. How will she respond as an adult to events that frighten her?

As an intuitive parent with children of different intuitive styles, Tara understands how children manage their environments or how the environmental influences affect the children. Her knowledge changes the way she handles situations to get effective results with her children. Her older son takes charge and her younger son is learning how to manage his empathic connection to other people's feelings.

Contrast environments for two brothers

Adam: Eleven-year-old Adam has strong physical intelligence. He is a baseball star and an athlete at heart. He is driven, confident, and determined in physical intelligence. He is also strong in intuitive intelligence. He reads other's feelings and responds or reacts, depending on the situation. Adam controls his environment through the use of his physical strengths and does not allow anyone or anything to control him.

For example, when Adam is challenged to a competition where he is not the expert, like in a chess game, he is determined to take control. He wants to create the circumstances he needs to excel at the activity. He will turn a "you can't …," into a challenge he will overcome.

When Adam feels the emotions of an unkind friend or tries out an activity in which he doesn't excel, he acts out his stress by being physically aggressive in some way. His learning task is to find positive outlets for his adrenaline. He needs constructive ways to manage his energy lest his physical strength become a weapon instead of his gift. Because Tara is aware of Adam's natural response to adverse environmental factors, she and her husband, Chris, are less prone to argue or take his actions personally. Instead, they direct his pent-up feelings through athletic activity or through communication where he expresses his frustration and discusses respect and disrespect. Adam can regulate his emotion quickly. Thus, here are characteristics of an intuitive child with strong physical intelligence like Adam.

- Maintains control of the surrounding environment to avoid being controlled by outside influences.
- Strong behavior patterns such as physical aggression or strong verbal communication (may be perceived as being mouthy or disrespectful).
- Can be triggered by upsetting situations and needs to manage effectively through a physical release so the emotion doesn't build up inside.

Caden: Seven-year-old Caden is the emotional intuitive, aware of the feelings of everyone around him. He is an empathic child, one who reacts to the emotional environment in a playgroup, school classroom, or with his siblings. In contrast to his brother who initiates action in his environment, Caden is more easily influenced by people and situations, internalizing it as a coping skill.

Often Caden comes home from school and within a short period of time has an emotional meltdown. Any parent might see the meltdown as normal kid behavior or the causes as trivial. The issues are not trivial to sensitive Caden. Tara and Chris accord him the importance of their time and efforts to soothe him and uncover the cause of his upset. The cause stems from what he witnesses, such as a friend being teased or hurt, or pain inflicted on another person or animal. He is particularly sensitive to violence.

Chris and Tara's parental challenge is to bring Caden back to his center and refocus his energies. Together, parents and Caden, monitor his warning signs of meltdown: irritability, aggression, or in some cases physical symptoms such as diarrhea or an upset stomach. Caden has learned to calm his sensitive nervous system before it builds up in his body and causes him further distress. Caden uses these techniques, which help him manage his emotions. He goes into the backyard in his bare feet and plays in the dirt. He plays in water, whether in a hot tub or pool. He plays independently on his gaming system away from his siblings, or he spends time alone in his room playing a relaxed, quiet game.

The contrast between the ways these two intuitive brothers interact with their environments opens parents' eyes. Once you observe how your intuitives negotiate their environments, you learn how to ease their journeys. You can see what skills to teach them to feel in control of their lives. The characteristics of an intuitive child coupled with strong emotional intelligence may be:

- Controlled by the emotions of the surrounding environment.
- Prone to intense emotional outbursts.
- Can have an adverse affect on the physical body.
- Needs to learn self-regulation by techniques that release the emotional energy from the physical body.

Chapter Review

Learning to negotiate new environments is especially beneficial to intuitive children because of their sensitivity to feelings, sound, stressors, people, and the mix of human emotions and behavior. How a child interacts with their environment is indicative of whether they make change happen or change happens to them, how they control or act on their environment or are controlled by it. Parents who are responsive, supportive, and empathic models of interaction correlate strongly with more confident children. Intuitive children have the best success when they are proactive, get results, and feel in control of their energy.

5

Parenting Styles and the Intuitive Child

Anyone can become angry. That is easy. But to he angry with the right person, to the right degree, at the right time, for the right purpose and in the right way—that is not easy.

—Aristotle

What is a parenting style?

A parenting style is *how* we interact with our children based on our own personality strengths and challenges. Each of us is born with a specific personal style or temperament that remains constant throughout our lives. Our consistent personal style guides the way we respond to people, tasks, and different environments. However, our teachers, life experiences, and environments shape who we become as we grow up and have our own children. This chapter explains how your parenting style interacts with intuitive children and why you get along well or clash.

Your parenting style affects your interactions

As parents, the task is to understand our children's personal styles, that is, how they learn and interact. We don't expect the child to conform to our styles. If they don't understand what we say or respond the way we want, then we have a disconnect. Our goal is to connect, to honor *how* they learn and process information. Thus, how we relate to our children depends on our personal characteristics:

- Are we outgoing and take charge of the environment?
- Are we inner focused and reactive to the world?
- Are we high achievers who do, do, do and expect our kids to jump right in?
- Are we thinkers who analyze all and explain everything to our kids? Do we fail to listen because we are too busy thinking?
- Are we harmonizers who love to keep the peace and overreact when disharmony prevails. Examples of disharmony include getting angry when children fight, play loud music, can't solve their own problems, or intrude on our personal time?
- Are we influencers who want our children to listen to us? Do we want to include them in our activities and be their friend?
- Like our intuitive children, are we feelers who are empathic with those around us? Do we have intuitive gifts to use in our parenting?

By understanding our own dominant traits and how we handle parenting situations with intuitive children, we'll better manage our reactions. We'll align more fully with our child's style for interacting with the world around them.

Understanding your parenting style clarifies *why* you have expectations of your intuitive child, or *how* you react when they don't meet your expectations. The following examples illustrate some common issues around parenting style clashes with intuitive children. The suggested solutions take into account the intuitive child's learning style, feelings, and values.

Parents who do and achieve

Parent doers are the planners who get things done without much discussion. They are strong role models of leadership for their children. They also model fearlessness and risk-taking. They expect kids to know how to do something without explaining it, and then wonder why their kids disappoint them. Not always sensitive to feelings of family members, especially children, they might overlook the small achievements, the creative process, or the daily report of school events. They might push kids too hard toward challenges and independence before they are ready.

High-achieving doers focus on tasks with an enviable persistence. Their challenges are to make time for the people in their lives, especially an intuitive child, and to consistently re-assess their priorities.

Example 1: If you are a doer who gets tasks done right away, you'll expect your intuitive child to hop to it when you say, "Take out the trash." Your intuitive child is coloring and daydreaming, and hasn't finished his drawing yet. You give a second order and expect movement from your child, and it doesn't happen. You have the choice to press the issue, creating anger around the situation and upsetting a sensitive child. Or you can decide to shift to his style, which includes allowing him time to finish the art project and not interrupting the daydreaming and then emptying the trash later. Ask questions: *When will you be done with your project? When you are done, I want you to take out the trash. Will you? Can I put this sticky note here as a reminder for you? Where can I put the sticky note so you will see it clearly and not forget? You will remember, yes?*

Example 2: Parents who are doers can be insensitive to children's feelings. Because intuitive children can be overly sensitive, they might perceive that they are in the wrong somehow. Seven-year-old Kathy ran into her mother's kitchen to share a weird experience of riding her bike too fast on the neighborhood sidewalk and hitting a neighbor's tree full force. Kathy flew off the bike and flipped a complete circle in the air before landing on the ground. The impact knocked out her breath, and she went flying into the sky. Suddenly, she was flying and looking down at her body. Then she flew back into her body and opened her eyes with so much adrenaline and excitement, she ran to tell her mom. Mom was busy cooking and said, "Not now

Kathy." The adrenaline bubbled out of Kathy's mouth uncontrollably, "But Mom I hit a tree and flew out of my body. I was in the sky." Doer Mom was busy, "I said not now, Kathy and I mean it. Go play." Kathy was still in adrenaline shock and a third attempt to share her flight was met with further rebuke. Solutions can be simple if a doer parent stops long enough at least to acknowledge her child. Don't brush her off. "I can't stop frying chicken right now, but I can listen. Go ahead." "If you will sit right there for five minutes, then I can sit with you, and you can tell about it." "Okay, I can't stop what I am doing, but you stir this slowly and tell me what happened, and I'll chop the onions.

Strengths of parents who do

- *Guide an intuitive child in experiential ways through demonstration.*
- *Give an intuitive child the authority in situations to learn to deal with responsibility.*
- *Model persistence for a child by sticking with the child to the end of a project or through a fearful situation.*
- *Invite participation in a project with set times for specific tasks.*

Parents who like harmony

Harmonizers or peacemakers like being close to their children and often claim that their children share most everything with them, even their secrets. They are honest and expect honesty. They acknowledge their children and honor their achievements, hurts, awards, and disappointments. They model how to value relationships and cooperation. The harmonizer is not always comfortable with arguing children, blasting music from their teen's room, back talk, rudeness, or interruptions while working or focused. The disruptions of household harmony, which triggers instability or dishonesty, are challenges for this parent.

Example 3: Your intuitive child is a sensitive boy who takes criticism personally. When teased by his older sister, he reacts with tears and fighting back. Moreover, this child comes to you to complain. Your child's complaints feed right into your sensitive heart, which wants peace and harmony.

Most sensitive parents react with bias toward the one who taunts, and may overprotect the intuitive. Or a parent who seeks peace and quiet may jump on both children. There are several solutions for helping children solve their own interactions that vary, based on your values.

You can listen to the complaining child, acknowledge the hurt feelings, and ask him how he would like to deal with it by helping him come up with options, choose one, and insure he follows through.

Remembering that intuitive children value appreciation of their experience, simple acknowledgement and listening may be enough. Before you end your interactions with your child, be sure to bring closure so the event doesn't dangle in his mind. "Are you over this now?" "Are you finished with this and ready to move on?" "Check your feelings to see if there is any more you need to express before moving on." "Are there last words you need to say before we close this matter?"

Guide the siblings through a sensitivity exercise to help them understand each other's styles. This usually works easily when they trade places with each other and close their eyes, imagining themselves as the sibling and feeling what they feel, then giving words to the feelings. Then guide their discussion to understanding their different styles.

If you remember that intuitive children, like all children, may seek to reconnect when feeling disconnected, your comfort may be enough without having to solve any problem. Your recognition of the child's need to let off steam is enough to release the hurt and move on.

As an empathic parent, check in with yourself to clarify if you are remaining neutral in blaming others for a child's hurt and helping the child to find ways to manage their feelings and solve their problems.

Gifts of parents who harmonize

- *Teach your intuitive child how to be **centered**.*
- *Offer nature walks as a way to develop **good feelings**.*
- *Help your child be **consistent** by setting goals and celebrating accomplishments.*
- *Use **touch** as a powerful bonding tool.*
- *Bring your child back to the **present** when she's worried or he's upset with a gentle reminder, "Be here now with me." You are here. Be present."*

Parents who analyze and think

Thinkers truly value talking and sharing with their children. From the time their child enters the world, analytical parents answer all questions and explain events. They are patient in instructing their children in life's how-tos. They might want their children to be experts on a topic or class assignment, making them dig deeper than is needed. Thinkers like perfection. Will their children measure up? The analyzing parent's challenge is to honor their intuitive child's learning style, which is experiential. Can analyzing parents shift from thinking to empathizing? Show them; don't tell them about it.

Example 4: Jalynn's intuitive daughter likes space in her room for different projects. The daughter has designated spaces in her small bedroom for writing, dress-up, painting, dancing, playing with her stuffed animals, studying, and reading. The parent walks into the bedroom and declares it a mess, and the daughter protests that each space is clearly designated. They clash. Mom wants the room cleaned up. Daughter wants her space and insists the spaces remain intact. The solution can involve both styles. Mom's style is to organize and clarify. Mom draws a scale replica of the room and invites her daughter to organize the space visually and to write down what she needs to "organize" it so it looks clean. Then Jalynn and her daughter shop for the organizers needed for the bedroom project. Daughter takes the scale model and "cleans" and organizes the paraphernalia in the spaces with her new baskets, drawers, and shelves.

Example 5: Cognitive dad loves coaching his son's little league team. He is careful to instruct his team members in the skills sets. He has over-criticized his son who lacks the athletic prowess and makes him a not-even-close-to-perfect specimen Dad would like to see. The intuitive son internalizes failure and quits trying to do well. The solution lies in Dad's acknowledgment of the intuitive's feelings and asking how is best to teach him: *How is it best for you to hold the bat? Do you want to work with me at home? Is there another Dad you like better to work with? What words do you want to hear me say that you feel are encouraging?*

Gifts of thinking-analyzing parents

- *Help your child **be thorough** by checking his homework, reading instructions carefully by demonstrating these study skills.*

- *Help your child **be cautious** in his choices by thinking through the consequences. Ask what might happen or instruct in listing consequences.*

- *Encourage **spirited debate** by brainstorming ideas, discussing issues, and honoring all analyses.*

- *When an intuitive child loses track of time, assist them in moving along, completing the task and responding to their environment.*

Parents who feel and influence

The parent is also an intuitive, who is sensitive to feelings and has ample opportunity to teach the intuitive child resilience. The influencer may try to escape stress and learn phenomenal coping skills to share. The feeling parent honors emotions and shares empathy without overindulgence. This parent teaches how to be of service and has the opportunity to model respect. This parent's challenge will be to help their intuitive children with structure and boundaries. Intuitive parents and children can be naïve and too trusting, so learning to listen to gut level feelings gains importance.

Example 6: Gail is an intuitive mom, whose son, Fred, is also a natural intuitive. Gail has worked consciously with her son to keep him in tune with his inner feelings, his wisdom. Gail refers to Fred as a "floater" among his peer group. He is a leader and has the ability to befriend anyone who has a genuine nature. He makes friends easily and doesn't judge them based on what others think. Fred is the first one to acknowledge someone else's achievement. Gail, however, sensitive to her own childhood intuitive experiences, pays close attention to how the children at this age interact, and it triggers emotions from her own upbringing.

Gail observes how Fred's friends, with whom he's played ball for years, have gravitated toward peer groups who are unkind and bullying. As difficult as it became for Gail, who experienced similar peers' behaviors, she had to watch her son be bullied by those he had befriended. Fred confided it wasn't so much the way they treated him that bothered him as much as how the kids pretended to be someone they weren't to impress other kids.

What Gail can do to help Fred set firm emotional boundaries with his peers is to examine her own feelings first. Gail projects her son's reactions based upon her hurt feelings when she was her son's age. Gail can acknowledge and validate what her son identifies about the kid's behavior that he dislikes.

Gail can also communicate with Fred about what he is feeling in a way that allows him to avoid internalizing the opinions of his peers. She can ask the question, "What is it exactly about Joe's behavior you do not like?"

Because Gail knows her son has a difficult time with lack of authenticity, she can comment by saying, "Sometimes kids aren't true to who they really are, because they are feeling insecure or something is bothering them which causes them to act in a way they may not otherwise act." She can follow up by asking, "Does that make sense?" to confirm her son understands what she is saying.

Gail can empower her son to remain authentic with himself when interacting with other kids. He can model genuineness. He doesn't have to conform to the group's opinion about someone.

Gifts of expressive feelers

- *Teach your child how to enjoy and **celebrate people**.*
- *Share how to listen to her body or **natural wisdom**.*
- *Share **performing service** and kind acts for others.*
- *Make time-outs a positive experience by sharing an orange, walking the dog, or laughing together **to ease tension**.*
- *Demonstrate respect for **friendships** and the value of **networking**.*

Chapter Review

Your parenting style is uniquely your own. Although each of us was born with a specific temperament that remains constant throughout our lives, our parents influenced how we parent today. So how you interact with your intuitive child may be a new experience.

Most parents will confess to intuitive episodes where information struck their senses with enough intensity to pay attention. Yet, many parents are very intuitive around children and don't realize how much they know. Whether you are a doer, a thinker, a harmonizer, or an intuitive in your parenting style, your goal is **to respond to the child in his or her style**. The next chapter provides helpful information about intuition at each stage of a child's life.

6

Intuition in Children Growing Up

How you choose to respond each moment to the movie of life determines how you see the next frame, and the next, and eventually how you feel when the movie ends.

—Doc Childre

How does intuition look?

Perhaps you know your child is intuitive or you suspect this is so and need clues. In the previous chapters, you've learned that intuitive intelligence is a specific way of relating to the world through experience, feelings, and sensitivity to people or the environment.

Intuitive children like to engage their environments directly, absorb information best through direct interactions. Ken Keis, CEO of Consulting Resource Group, explained that intuitive learners follow an inner flow of their own thoughts and ideas. Such a child is not easily contained in a school desk when they need freedom of movement and exploration. Their minds are curious and creative and often create some great entrepreneurial ideas. Educational systems that offer exploration, movement, drama, writing, games of pretend, and problem-solving are better alternatives for intuitive children. Teachers who allow time for discussion, daydreaming, creative expression, and movement have more success with intuitive children than traditional teachers.

An intuitive child is sensitive to the feelings of others. They read emotions and sense another's moods empathically. If feelings are overwhelming, then intuitive children need guidance in recognizing the warning signs of distress to manage their emotions and attitudes. Our goal for intuitive children is to equip them to know themselves inside and out. Another goal is that they engage their environment by taking charge, not always being reactionary.

Intuitive children may be psychic. This means that the physical world, the non-physical world, and the spiritual world blend together into one reality. They can see, hear, feel, and know the non-physical as well as the physical. Here are some examples at different ages.

1. Nine-month-old Emma laughs and waves to her angels in the corner of her bedroom, which her dad only feels as a peaceful energy.

2. Maureen's best friend died in a car accident when they were freshman in high school. Shortly after her friend's funeral, Maureen saw her friend each night before she went to sleep. Her friend shared what it was like to pass over into the non-physical world and how she was adjusting.

3. Eighteen-year-old Tim, a true explorer at heart, liked to ride his motorcycle all over the countryside, and he noticed a peculiar pattern. He felt nauseous at certain times and stopped his bike on the roadside. At these moments, he closed his eyes and felt impressions of accidents on the highway. He felt the energy vibes of traumatic events. Eventually he documented some of these by exploring local newspapers. At other times he pulled over when he saw a marker, like flowers or a cross, noting that someone had died in an accident at that spot.

4. Ten-year-old James told his mother that some "weird" person was watching his friend and him at the playground. James said the man felt icky to him. His mom believed him and joined the kids for a game of soccer and alerted the police when she saw the man hovering nearby. The man was listed in the registry of sex offenders as a pedophile.

5. Four-year-old Caden didn't understand why his grandpa didn't respond to his knock on the casket at his funeral. To Caden, grandpa was in the room with the rest of the people, but he was the only one who could see him. Caden would see his grandpa everyday for several more years and would describe to his parents the different things grandpa was doing in the other dimension.

Intuition through children's development

Each intelligence or ability…is a potential brought into our awareness through neural circuits in our brain as those circuits respond to stimuli of like order from the environment.

—James Chilton Pearce (*Evolutions' End*, 1992)

The knowledge of what to look for in children with regard to intuitive intelligence is helpful. You'll find in the following stages ways to nurture a child's natural intelligence. As children develop through the toddler, pre-school, elementary, tween, and teen stages, how do they demonstrate intuitive intelligence?

Toddlers—preverbal children act out their connections to their parents and caregivers. Because babies and toddlers watch us and process our feelings and reactions, as a parent you want to observe and take note of how your child expresses feelings and approaches his environment.

- Natalie at four to six months of age cried every time another baby cried in the infant massage class attended by six moms and their children. She showed empathy at another baby's crying.

- One-year-old James threw a small toy truck at his mom when she lay on the couch with the flu. He felt her discomfort and noted she was different. Mom knew James felt disconnected from her and invited him to be on the couch with her. His acting out behavior stopped when he felt reconnected.

- Babies and toddlers need movement as in being carried in slings, rocked in the swing, rolled around on the couch, sliding along the floor, or pushing toys. All of this movement is to develop neurons for orienting their body in space, learning balance, motor skills, and training the nervous system in movement. All children learn from feedback from their muscles, tendons, and movement. Intuitive children can be especially sensitive to movement and feelings in their bodies as they mature. Babies and toddlers are about sensation, feeling, impression, body moving, and exploring instinctually.

- Repetitious actions such as banging on a drum, going down the slide a dozen times, running in circles, and pushing a button to hear the same rhythm repeatedly are all part of a toddler's negotiating his or her terrain. By completing cycles of such rhythmic play, the brain develops neural pathways. The baby learns concentration and focus. If dad yells at the child to stop, the child doesn't hear because his brain is doing what it is supposed to do, repeat patterns. The child is completely absorbed. However, a smack interrupts the child's cycle of attention. Now the child has stopped, but the child is leery of the environment. In addition he cannot now do one task to train his brain; he now has to watch out for two environments. This doesn't work for a sensitive or intuitive child. When they grow up and say I cannot concentrate, remember this message. The reptilian and limbic systems are best trained in a safe environment that encourages natural exploration, play, and interaction that is positive.

- Around the age of 18 months to 3 years, the limbic brain, our emotional system, develops and compels the toddler to explore, to act upon the environment. Just as the baby was sensation, the toddler is all emotions and intuition. (Not emotional, just emotion.) Emotion must express itself through the body, and as a parent, your job is *not* to take it personally. Your child is not doing it to you. Rather, provide gentle redirection of behavior, touch, and calming, a safe room for the tantrum. Punishment, directed parental anger and inflicting physical pain will teach your child to not act on the environment, but rather retreat because it hurts. Moreover, you hurt! Your rage, anger, and intensity make your child feel ill. You are no longer safe and the environment is no longer safe. This becomes claustrophobic or suffocating for a sensitive child and becomes hardwired into the brain system, which compels a child forward to persevere within the environment,

Preschoolers can discern the physical, nonphysical, and spiritual worlds as one reality.

- Jean Piaget felt intuition developed around age 4. By now, you'll have a sense of your child's level of sensitivity as well as how much they focus on the images and beings of the nonphysical world. Their focus on the non-physical world sharpens, as does their ability to articulate it at this age.

- At this age, the emotional brain develops deep, thicker connections with the right-brain hemisphere. The left brain is analytical and focused in time and structure. The right brain is holographic, open to the energy of space, spirit, or universe, whichever word you use. Preschoolers mostly live in both worlds.

- Just like a cat or dog will act nervous, whine, and be jumpy before an earthquake because they sense it, preschoolers also sense vibrations of the people and activities in their environment. Their world consists of the physical and nonphysical worlds, and in many cases the spiritual world. Children report imaginary friends, scary ghosts, friendly ghosts, dead relatives who relay messages or play games with them, angels who help them, and extraterrestrials who teach them.

- Some children at this age are able to leave their body and go to another place. They may remember and share these dreams with you. As a parent, how will you listen and acknowledge their experiences?

- Let's remember that preschoolers with intuitive intelligence can have rich imaginations and not be psychic at all. Their rich fantasy and highly creative play can occupy them for hours, is fun, and may translate into daydreaming as they grow older.

- Of critical importance in these preschool years is children's emotional and mental health—that they feel safe and believe they are safe. If the environment is not safe, then their learning shifts to survival instead of exploring and learning. In these preschool years, more parents and grandparents take their children to psychiatrists and pediatricians to understand why their child is seeing a ghost or acting out imaginary super hero games! These are normal and do not require medical intervention. Your choices will be to put the child on unregulated adult medications or hang with the child and see how their gift progresses.

The imaginary friend

Wendy shares a story of her intuitive connection to her daughter, Jillian:

When I was pregnant with my daughter, I knew that she was a girl, which was exciting for my family. My daughter, Jillian, was the first grandchild in my family. I knew she would have dark hair and dark eyes, all of which she had. My Jillian was born on May 20th.

I was closest to my mother-in-law when Jillian was born, and I could turn to her for advice. Yet, I raised Jillian through my intuition. Nobody believed that I was a first-time mother with Jillian, because I wasn't a typical, nervous mother. I was calm and confident because of my intuition with her.

Jillian was an early talker and a sweet, outgoing, little girl. From a young age, she was creative and imaginative. She enjoyed playing by herself or being in play groups. At age 3, Jillian had an imaginary friend named Timmy. Wherever we walked, Timmy walked with us. In fact he was always with us. My in-laws thought we were nuts. At first, my husband thought the whole incident was crazy, but he went along with it. Timmy was in the car with us, went shopping with us, and enjoyed our family dinners.

I wanted the family to embrace Timmy, and they did. Whatever their own personal feelings about the imaginary friend, they listened to me when I said, "Jillian can have Timmy. Timmy is real to her, and I don't think there's anything wrong with that. Timmy was in our lives for three years, and then he disappeared one day.

When Jillian was four, her grandmother died. One morning some time later, Jillian woke up and said to me, "Gee Gee was with me last night. Gee Gee came into my room.

I said, "Really? What did Gee Gee say?"

"Well, she didn't say anything; she just smiled at me."

"See, I told you. Gee Gee is always around us. She's here." And I always felt that Gee Gee spoke to me, and I shared it with her family. Also Gee Gee visited Jillian several more times.

Throughout my years of being a mom, I have always taken into account my children's feelings and realizing the importance of respecting them and respecting their feelings. As Jillian grew up, I've had bad feelings about some of her friends. This is a difficult place for an intuitive parent to be. I said to my husband, "You know, I don't like this situation. I don't like this friend that Jillian has made. I have a very bad sense about this person."

He forced me to step back and not impart my feelings to Jillian, as she had to find her way. The way I approached it was, when she spoke to me about this friend, I would listen and then say, "Well, you know Jillian, how about thinking of it this way? What do you think they're trying to gain by behaving that way or treating you that way?" Through time, her eyes opened, because this friend wasn't respecting her and had issues and problems. Then the situation blew up in our faces. Howard said to me, "My god, why didn't I listen to you?"

Sometimes, being an intuitive parent is difficult, because I knew I was right. Yet, there is always the question of whether a parent takes control. I knew that Jillian had to find this out on her own. I think part of growing up is having to go through some of the hard knocks to build character, strength, and resilience. Today Jillian and I can talk about this situation openly, and she admits to what I knew so many years ago.

Childhood

- If intuitives received support and interest from their environments as a preschooler, then they progress in their specific gifts, whether creativity, artistic inspiration, enjoying people, or seeing beyond. Linear thinking, moving into cognition, or intellectual development happens around ages 6 and 7. At this time intuitive intelligence can take a back seat. Psychic gifts, if not utilized or supported, extinguish themselves.

- If psychic gifts are supported and children are still empathic, creative, or interacting with the world beyond, then the child has words to explain why the ghost is visiting and even what the colors around your body are.

- Children who are especially empathic with animals might communicate with them in pictures and feel bonded to them strongly.

- If nature calls to your child, your intuitive might see fairies around flowers or that mountains appear as giant angels because they feel strongly connected to the Earth.

- By this time, creative intuitive children are finding a love for an art form such as dancing, music, drama, painting, or gymnastics.

- Children with emotional empathy may find these years more difficult. They want to keep their sensitivity, yet they may believe other intellectual children or teachers who tell them it is time to put their imagination away and get on with life. They could feel pulled between their rich emotional life and their intellectual common sense. In later chapters, you'll find specific activities about how empathic children can balance their head and heart to make good decisions.

- Childhood years are about cognitive development. It is an opportune time for telepathy to increase. However, interactions with the nonphysical world or spiritual world will either cease or come into harmony as the child can grasp how it works and why he has a talent and what to do with it.

- Emotionally sensitive and empathic children can become more volatile as new cognition and discovery vie for importance. Now is the time to model (if you haven't already) self-management tools presented in later chapters. Mostly, you have to do the exercises with your child for a while if they are to believe them important or helpful. If you do not value them for yourself, neither will they.

- The childhood years are a phenomenal time for the intuitive artistic mind. Intuitive children like exploring the arts for expressing their creativity. Painting, dancing, sculpting, swimming—what would your artistic child like to do? When they tell you, be sure to listen to the real message. When Caron's 8-year-old daughter said, "I want to paint," Caron jumped on it. She found an instructor, bought the supplies, and attended the first session with her daughter. The first session was okay, and in the second and third sessions, the daughter was getting rebellious. Caron asked why, and her daughter said, "I want to paint, I don't want a teacher." Ohhhh! The light dawned. So her daughter, without instruction, painted and loved it. She had found her niche.

Chapter Review

Children's intuition displays prominently in their toddler and preschool years. Their intuitive intelligence can also show up in a specific interest in an activity. In research studies, infants who are empathic have demonstrated concern or modeling crying or distress signals when feeling another's distress. Preschoolers brainwave patterns indicate they are in a relaxed, yet alert state as they learn to negotiate their environment. A safe environment in which a loving adult meets their needs is mandatory for the building of self-confidence and security. This is an opportune time for connection with the nonphysical world.

Intellectual development starts around school age, and can enhance intuitive skills or motivate the child in a different direction.

7

Intuition in the Tween and Teen Years

You cannot depend on your eyes when your imagination is out of focus.
—Mark Twain

This chapter continues our discussion of how intuitive intelligence might unfold through children's maturity. We'll discuss pubescence, or tweens and teens.

Tween years

The tween years are normally labeled pubescence and occur roughly between 8 and 9 to 11 or 12.

In Caron's professional work as a teacher and later as a psychotherapist and spiritual counselor, she's observed that intuitive tweens also have eyes and ears that reach into the nonphysical world and the spiritual realm. After the cognitive growth and creative capacities in their childhood phase, tweens have to check with themselves and ask, "Do I really want to close the door on these intuitive gifts before the brain reorganizes itself when I am a teen?"

To the psychic pubescent who wants to keep these gifts open, similar experiences that occurred in their preschool years may reoccur. Ghosts appear, telepathy between close friends or networks of friends increases, telekinesis increases, and conversations with inner teachers can provide strength and clarity. Psychic children who were precognitive may find their dreams more lucid and predictive ability increased.

The creative energy soars also for the artistic intuitive. This is a time of dreaming their futures, writing poetry, practicing to be the next drama queen, or discovering the cure for cancer. Futures are created in the pubescent years.

Emotionally empathic tweens may have the hardest time in these years of peer groups who define their standards. Empathic intuitives will feel more deeply in the pubescent years, and peer groups could be helpful or harmful.

Samantha's story

Samantha is an empathic intuitive tween who can feel the emotions of the people around her. Specifically, she is strongly connected to her sister Jan, and often will run Jan's energy. Jan has battled bouts of depression and Samantha has shared that she can see the gray clouds that cluster around Jan's energy field.

Jan shares her viewpoint: "When I started middle school, my best friend of many years would no longer speak to me. I also became aware of some of the other kids' energy at school and have experienced being picked on at the bus stop.

"A few years ago, my sister Jan was hospitalized for clinical depression and has been emotionally unstable since. I used to be able to talk to Jan about peer experiences, as she is older than I am and has been through a lot of it already.

"Because I can feel Jan's emotions, I know I can no longer discuss these things with her and I feel sad. There was a situation where I did tell Jan what one of the girls on the bus called me and she became enraged. It scared me, so I am afraid now to talk to her about these kinds of situations for fear she will be hospitalized again."

If intuitive children could form coalitions with other intuitive children, they would find strength in numbers and familiar friends with whom to discuss their feelings and phenomena.

In these years children will decide whether or not to keep their sensitivity open or refocus their life in another direction in adolescence. Much of their choice will depend upon parental support and guidance.

Adolescents turn the futuristic life of the tween into an idealized version for their future. An adolescent needs the answers to existential questions, "Why am I here? What is my purpose? Who am I?" They need a model of authenticity and greatness to be able to focus their intention and actions for their futures.

The intuition of a teenager can provide the wisdom and guidance to help focus direction. In addition, this wisdom needs a solid set of values so a teen can say, "This is what I stand for!"

Now would be the ideal time to model trust in the inner voice paired with goals and common sense. Teach your children the value of listening to that inner wisdom, through their internal trust walk.

We present a word of caution to empower the teen to believe and achieve their dream, and remain with two feet on the ground.

An empathic teen feels disappointment, depression, and peer group pressure more deeply than most. Teens by now should have mood management skills.

Sensitive teens need mentors to transform their energy into the most productive and passionate activities.

An intuitive's mind

In this example Tara talks with her son Adam, an intuitive adolescent, about the impact violent video games has on the mind and how it can desensitize his intuitive connection. Adam can remain open in his intuition with more productive activities.

Tara shares:

My oldest son, Adam, and I were on one of our Sunday walks when he raised this question: "Why can't I play the video games my friends can play?" Of course I knew he was referring to the violent, shoot-'em-up variety, which are absolutely forbidden in our house, but I decided to turn this into an impressionable conversation.

The road we live on is a beautiful country road that winds through the Blue Ridge Mountains in Virginia. Everywhere you look there are sprawling hills and beautiful vegetation. There are many horse farms and other forms of wildlife, which further enhances the beauty of the landscape. I stopped in front of one of the many 50-acre horse farms and began to paint a picture for my son.

Look around at everything—the trees, the sky, horses, cows, birds, grass, a barn, ducks. Now imagine that everything you see right now is being photographed by your mind. At any time you may see a flash of this landscape because somewhere in your brain, these pictures have been downloaded like photos on a computer; these images can be called on at any moment. If you stood here and looked at this view every day and meditated on its beauty, you would eventually be able to pull up the visual image you see now, at any moment. You would get to the point where anytime you closed your eyes and imagined this picture in your mind, you would also feel calm and peaceful, just like you do now. Your brain has associated this feeling with this image.

Your brain also associates the excited, aggressive feeling with the violent images on video games. The more time you spend in front of violent games, the more you pull up those images in your mind. For some children, this has influenced their behavior, leading them to do things they may not have otherwise done. Violence, when made a part of a child's life before their brain fully develops, which is around age 25, desensitizes their ability to connect with the inner knowing we all have of what's right and wrong.

In Dr. Spock's book, Baby and Child Care, 8th Edition *(Pocket Books, 2004), he writes:*

"As technology improves and the screens become more and more lifelike, children shoot at images that look increasingly like real people. The more they shoot, the less horror and disgust they feel at the idea of killing people. It's not that they become cold-blooded exactly, just less tenderhearted. When they think of flying bullets, their main emotion is excitement, not fear or revulsion. Video games, much more than violent movies, have the ability to capture children's imaginations and train their emotions to accept violence, because with video games children are active participants."

Tara's and Adam's conversation continues

Adam looked at me wide-eyed, and I knew in that moment, he completely and fully understood what I had explained to him. Intuitively he got it. For me, it was a great accomplishment, because anytime an intuitive connection can be linked to a more productive way of using one's time, I feel it's a success.

Later that evening while headed to a neighbor's house, we passed the same spot we had stopped to have our discussion and Adam said, "Mom, remember the picture?" I smiled, because it confirmed he heard what I said.

I remember a statement my mom made once upon a time, which I didn't really understand until now: "What we put into our mind through vehicles such as television and other forms of media carry energy, which can manifest into things in our experience." As I have evolved, I have come to know this more as truth.

What teens need

In our years of working with teens, they have made their needs clear regarding their intuitive intelligence. This is our laundry list for parents of intuitive teens:

- Quiet time for reflection.
- Appreciation for who they are as individuals.
- Not to be afraid of their talents or their power.
- A mentor who listens and encourages their creativity.
- Creative projects or service projects to focus attention on the value of giving and sharing.

- Someone who complements his or her traits.
- Someone who celebrates their achievements.
- Money management.
- Exploration of transcendence and consciousness.
- Parents who still expect boundaries.
- Parents who try to understand their viewpoints.

There are only two lasting bequests we can hope to give our children. One is roots; the other, wings.

—Hodding Carter

Intuition for adolescents, as we have learned, could be one of the more difficult times without parental support. Tara continues her discussion of Adam's intuition here through a conversation she and her son had shortly before the publication of this book. The conversation demonstrates how children who are given a strong spiritual foundation, along with the freedom to exercise what they have been taught, will make choices based on what triggers their intuitive knowing.

Tara shares:

"I was at a PTO meeting at Adam's middle school when one of the dad's we know made a comment, "Yeah I need to talk to you about your son." Immediately I could feel the energy rush inside of me. I sat and wondered for the next two hours what he could possibly need to talk to Chris and I about. Adam is a good kid and typically doesn't do anything I would worry about."

She continued, "In fact, just that week, a mother came up to me at our younger son's baseball game and shared that as a fifth grade teacher, it made her feel good to know there are normal sixth graders out there and commented on how polite and helpful Adam was with the little kids at the playground. I felt proud that another mother recognized his behavior and shared her thoughts.

"So after the PTO meeting I approached the dad and asked what he meant. By that time, he had forgotten he made the comment and mentioned that his son had made a comment regarding some language Adam had used. Naturally, I was playing the scene in my head—how he would lose his cell phone; what boundaries would I put in place to curb the inappropriate talk; what were the reasons Adam had for saying things he knows better than to say; not my son...

"I was calm when we arrived home, but as soon as I walked in I said to Adam, We need to talk." Immediately, his face turned beet red and he became nervous, mainly because my tone was calm, but serious. He asked if he was in trouble, and I replied he wouldn't be if he answered my questions honestly. We sat down and had what became one of our most intuitive conversations yet.

"I asked him what kinds of things he was saying in school that would be construed as inappropriate. He confessed without hesitation that he had said some things he knew weren't acceptable. What impressed me was his ability to convey his reasoning for it.

"Mom, I am expressing my feelings."

"I understand that Adam, but there are appropriate ways to speak your emotions and things you shouldn't say. What is causing you to feel this way?"

"Some of the kids are being mean to other kids and it makes me mad. Mom, I can feel what they're thinking and I don't like it. I am actually acting out their energy."

"Why don't you consider writing your thoughts in a journal rather than speaking them out loud?"

"Mom, I would never write these words down, it makes them worse."

"I couldn't argue with his assessment of the situation, because when I was his age I could feel the exact same energy he was describing. I could feel what the other kids were thinking and often times reflected it through my behavior as well.

"We continued our conversation for quite a while as I recommended ways he could handle his emotions without cussing or saying inappropriate things. We also discussed how this is yet another way kids his age are desensitized to language because of all of the ways they are exposed to it. Parents hear what comes out of their child's mouth.

"I respect Adam for intuitively knowing what was bothering him, how he was reacting to it, and how he knew he could express his feelings openly and honestly with me.

"I have also noticed how the more he relies on his intuition, the more he is pulling back from some of the choices his friends are making. Initially, when he started middle school, he was completely absorbed in all of the girls he was meeting; all of the people he was texting; going to football games with his friends; time spent downstairs playing Xbox or watching T.V.; loss of interest in his school work and baseball. He was on the go with his friends that initially caused me some emotional struggle, because I felt I was losing some connection with him, although I was prepared to let go.

"I had to accept he was growing up, but all of a sudden, he is up in the family room with us at night. He is striving to get A's on his school work and he commented about how his friends are more interested in girls than baseball, but he's not anymore. He isn't asking to go to football games at night, and he has rekindled his puppy love for the girl he has liked since first grade. I have seen a total transformation back to his inner truth."

When an intuitive child has a strong spiritual foundation, as we see with Tara's son Adam, they will naturally pull away and curiously try new things. However, if they feel it goes against their inner truth, with the proper management skills, they will naturally realign with their intuitive self.

As an intuitive parent, Tara has given her son the freedom he needed to experience new things, but she has also given him the tools he needs to manage the choices he makes. When he felt divided within himself, he relied on the strength of his intuitive intelligence to pull back, and felt connected enough with his mom to share his emotions.

Chapter Review

Intuition is the knowing sense. All of us have the capacity, and some children and teens have intuitive intelligence that manifests as emotional empathy, creative artistry, or psychic gifts. Our human brains—reptilian, limbic, neocortex, and frontal cortex—provide direction for the developmental stages through which we pass. Intuition and our connection to the other worlds are stronger in the preschool and pubescent years. In the teen years, intuitive intelligence can guide adolescents to determining their values and intentions for the next stage of their lives, and a mentor or model in the intuitive field can strengthen one's inner trust.

8

Intuitive Children and Environmental Toxicity

Some misfortunes we bring upon ourselves; others are completely beyond our control. But no matter what happens to us, we always have some control over what we do about it.

—Suzy Szasz

We live in phenomenal times when whole-brain function and use of intuition are at the forefront. Simultaneously, we are living with unparalleled global toxicity, which poisons our inner terrain, damages immune systems, and produces unprecedented rates of illness. And the illnesses are not short-term. The illnesses our children live with today are life-long commitments that established medical procedures can manage, but not cure. Humans' left-brain directives, during the last 100 years, have compromised the Earth's immune system as well as ours. Now truly is the time for extraordinary immune systems, vigorous health, active bodies, and sharp, clear minds.

Thus enters intuition as a model for negotiating our natural environments with ease and following our bodies' guidance about its needs, treatments, activity, and foods (all of which we cover in later chapters). For now, please read the summaries of the environmental situations in this chapter. We know the news and radio bombards you about it, probably to the point of tuning out. If your personal style is the Doer, then you are or will do something about it. But 75 percent of us won't do anything about preventive measures or establishing healthy lifestyles because it overwhelms us. We don't know where to start and we are too tired to make an extra effort. As a concerned parent, it's critical that you become informed of the very real dangers of the many environmental toxins that surround your family, and educate yourself about the steps you can take to keep your child safe.

Here is where you start. As you read the environmental stats, see which section makes you angry or irritated. If specific information unsettles you, that's a good sign. If air pollution pisses you off, then clean air is your cause. You value that. Take action by starting in your home, with your health and that of your children.

Toxicity builds in the human body

The EPA estimates that there are more than 20,000 chemicals our bodies cannot metabolize. When the human body fails to metabolize (and subsequently purge) these substances, the only alternative available is for the body to process the compounds via the liver, and then store the toxic elements in fat cells.[1] This cycle is known as bioaccumulation, and is a subject of increasing study by scientists around the world. Studies show that most people have between 400 and 800 different chemical residues stored within the cells of their bodies. One study in particular conducted by the EPA revealed that 100 percent of the tested subjects had dioxins, PCB's, dichlorobenzene, and xylene stored in their fat cells. Additionally, examination of their breath revealed that 89 percent had residual traces of carcinogenic benzene and 93 percent had traces of percholeathylene.[2]

How did people become so toxic? Although the past hundred years have seen remarkable scientific and industrial advances, this burgeoning technology also brought with it a detrimental consequence—society's movement away from the use of natural substances and instead becoming reliant on manufactured and synthetic goods.[3]

From the food and water we consume to the air we breathe, children today are bombarded with environmental toxins like no previous generation before them. And while this in and of itself is frightening, the far more alarming concern for parents is the disparity between children and adults regarding their susceptibility to environmental toxins.

Environmental pollution

Emotional, empathic, or sensitive children may have nervous systems and immune systems that are more susceptible or reactionary than children with other intelligences like physical strengths. Reactionary immune systems create hypersensitive reactions to environmental toxicity, which results in allergies, asthma, and compromised immune systems. The following facts aren't pretty, but they are real, and we can no longer turn blind eyes to relevant factors that influence our children's health.

Exposure begins in utero, and continues unabated throughout puberty and adolescence via a variety of sources, including the food we eat, the water we drink, the air we breathe, as well as from everyday environmental exposure in homes, schools, and even on playgrounds and athletic fields.

In North America, more than 77,000 synthetic chemicals are actively manufactured,[4] including combinations of 900 pesticide chemicals that are used to create more than 20,000 pesticide products.[5] A large majority of these chemicals have not been fully tested for health and environmental effects, and a National Academy of Sciences study found that 78 percent of the most heavily used chemicals in commercial applications had not even undergone "minimal" toxicity testing.[6]

In essence, our children are besieged by an onslaught of toxicity that impacts not only their development, but also their long-term health into adulthood. Problems associated with environmental toxins include neurological disorders, learning difficulties, birth defects, reproductive harm, immune toxicity, asthma and respiratory disorders, endocrine system dysfunction, and cancer.[7]

Natural cleaning products

The incidence of chemical exposure within our own homes is frightening, and commercial cleaning products contain a host of substances that can impact our children and increase the environmental toxicity in their young lives.

Two natural products have been mainstays in the cleaning arsenal for countless of previous generations of moms. Baking soda and vinegar are pantry staples in most homes, and both do a superb job of cleaning in a toxic-free manner.

Vinegar can be mixed with water on a 1:1 ratio and used as an all-purpose cleaner throughout the home. To clean toilet bowls, opt for a 100-percent vinegar solution directly on bowl surfaces and then scrub as usual with a toilet brush.

Baking soda is another item most people have on hand, and can be used as a substitute for harsh abrasives. Use it to clean your sink or stove, and as a deodorizer in refrigerators and closets.

Lemons are also a fresh alternative to chemical cleaners. Not only do they leave a clean and fresh scent, but they serve multiple purposes when combined with other ingredients. You can make a natural, homemade furniture polish by combining 1 cup of olive oil with a half cup of lemon juice. You can also pour baking soda on lemon slices and then use them to scrub deposits on dishes and pans (and you won't have to worry about chemical residues on plates that are in direct contact with the food your family eats).

Environmental toxicity is a real threat, one that is growing exponentially with every passing generation. As a parent, it's up to you to take steps to help protect your child, and there are a variety of ways in which you can do this. At first it may seem overwhelming. How can parents realistically protect children when the world is filled with chemicals and pesticides and a slew of other environmental toxins? By shielding your child in her everyday environments of home, school, and athletic fields, you increase her tolerance to combat the remaining environmental toxins she is bound to encounter.[8]

A parent's intuition knows

At the core of Tara's parenting is her children's health. Tara recounts her story: "When my oldest son, Adam, was young, I felt strongly about eliminating any foods with preservatives, dyes, hormones or antibiotics, or artificial ingredients (including sodas) from our diet. I couldn't really say why I felt so strongly, but something inside encouraged me to make these changes, and so I trusted my intuition in the matter.

"Today we are aware that most of these things impact the health, weight, or behavior of our children. To further support my intuitive nudges, at the age of 32, I found out I had an intolerance to gluten. The early signs were fatigue, cramping in my intestines, which produced a lot of gas and gas pains, and irregular bowel movements for a day or two after eating bread or other wheat-based products. Not long after that, my husband found out he was gluten intolerant and so was our 2-year-old daughter. In fact, our daughter has intolerances to lactose, gluten, and certain grains, and our doctor concluded probably a few other allergies we aren't aware of at this time. The physical signs that indicated to me she was suffering from these same allergies were discomfort in her stomach, the gas she passed at such a young age, and the distress she experienced when going to the bathroom."

Organic and Raw Food: Although we often don't have control of many environmental factors, diet is one area in which we have almost 100-percent control. One of the easiest ways to reduce risk of exposure to environmental toxins is by eating organic food.[9] The term "organic" is regulated by the USDA, and indicates that the food has been grown or produced without pesticides, fertilizers, ionizing radiation, or food additives.

Luckily, the movement towards "going organic" is growing. Not only are there entire organic and natural foods supermarkets, but most mainstream grocery stores also feature sections devoted entirely to organic foods and produce.

You can also minimize exposure to carcinogens by opting to eat vegetables in their natural raw state, and by cooking meats at lower temperatures for longer periods of time. If you love to barbeque, save it for special occasions and again cook the food longer at lower temperatures.[10]

A note on bottled water: Water continues to be a source of environmental toxicity both in lakes and streams as well as aquifers. Bottled water is one alternative, but you need to do your homework and read labels carefully. Although up to 75 percent of bottled waters come from springs and artesian wells, up to 25 percent of brands of bottled water are merely purified forms of water from municipal water sources.[11]

Tara continues:

My values regarding health caused me to question my children's need for vaccinations, antibiotics for treating ailments such as ear infections or colds, and chemicals in our everyday products such as laundry soap and cleaning supplies. Believe me when I tell you that I had a difficult time standing in the pediatrician's office and declining a vaccination. They will attempt everything to convince you why they know what's best. When my gut screamed no, I had to trust my answer. In the end, I stuck with my gut feeling. Since that time there have been several cases of autism linked to certain vaccinations and although a majority of the medical community and the pharmaceutical companies will do their best to discredit these findings, my intuition says otherwise.

Which vaccinations my children take come directly from my intuitive feelings about each child's constitution. A recent example of this occurred with Adam's entrance into middle school. They require that the kids are up-to-date on their tetanus shot, which I support. However, I discovered that they wanted the Tdap (tetanus, diphtheria, pertussis) shot renewed within the previous five years. His shot was administered six years ago. In this situation, I did not feel it was necessary to give him another shot for something he shouldn't need to have updated for at least two more years.

In other words, in the eyes of the healthcare system Adam is vaccinated until the age of 13, but the school wants to add extra protection by requiring that their shots be within five years, adding another dosage of something to his system he shouldn't need for two more years. I politely declined their request, which requires that our doctor send the school a signed form stating this is our position on the matter. In situations such as these, our children need us to be advocates for their health and well being. Trusting our intuitive nudges is the first step in the process.

My child's health scare

Tara's story continues:

I was cutting 11-year-old Adam's hair one afternoon when I found a reddish colored mark on his head. I made a mental note to show it to the doctor at Adam's next school physical. I asked Adam whether he had noticed it before, and he said it had been there for a few months. He has thick hair and wears baseball hats much of the time.

At Adam's doctor's appointment, I showed the doctor a pinkish red mark I had discovered on the back of my arm. He glanced at it, immediately diagnosed it as a carcinoma and encouraged me to schedule a biopsy to have it removed. I scheduled my appointment and on our way home, Adam brought up the spot on his head.

My heart dropped. I could not believe I had forgotten to show the doctor Adam's mark. My forgetfulness turned to fear when I realized the mark on Adam's head looked like the mark on my arm. Fear turned to panic at the thought of my son having skin cancer on his head.

The next morning, with tears in my eyes, I anxiously called the doctor with the hope of scheduling an appointment for Adam's head to coincide with my appointment. Fortunately, they were able to see him at the same time.

Being a health conscious person, the first question I ask myself is, "What inner changes need to be made to counteract what showed up on my outer body, the skin?" Knowing the small patch of cancer was a warning of imbalance inside, I took further action to create better internal balance. I found vitamins containing high doses of antioxidant rich green vegetables, high concentrations of fruits such as blueberries, pomegranates, or red grapes (also known as foods high in polyphenols), DHA from fish oil, and an oil salve made of Buckthorn which I applied to Adam's head and my skin twice a day.

My own research uncovered what food items would sustain our immune health, which included dark colored fruits and vegetables. Intuition said to stay away from high levels of sugar, refined products, and processed foods.

Given I am not a parent who allows my children to eat processed foods or drink sugary sodas or beverages, I was still shocked by the carcinoma diagnosis and my fear for Adam.

Food myth

Did you know that the term *processed* is not exclusive to canned, artificial, packaged, or chemically altered foods? In fact, any food item, which is prepared and reaches a temperature above 109 degrees, is considered processed. What does this mean for you and your family? The moment food reaches a temperature that exceeds 109 degrees, digestive enzymes which naturally break down fats, sugars, and proteins begin to have less of an affect on the body's natural abilities to break down food.

In one famous study regarding the importance of food enzymes, Dr. Francis M. Pottenger, Jr., worked with approximately 900 cats during a period of 10 years and studied how diet impacted their health and well being. He separated the cats into groups, and placed each group on one of five different diets, with each group receiving varying amounts of raw meat, milk products, and cod liver oil. Pottenger's findings documented that the cats fared best on a diet of raw milk and raw meat, which gave them optimal health. The cats in the remaining groups who drank varieties of milk other than raw had significant health problems, including degenerative bone disease, increased allergies, adverse personality changes, and even infertility.[12]

Indoor air quality

There is much you can do to help control the indoor air quality of your home. From opting to use hardwood or tiled flooring instead of fiber-based carpeting and rugs, you can limit not only the chemicals used in manufacturing the carpeting, but also eliminate a prime source that traps allergens in your home.

Indoor air filters are another option. Before you purchase one, however, take the time to research both the level of pollution it can remove from the air, as well as the air capacity of what it cleans (you want high levels for both figures).

Cleaning the air ducts of your home should be a quarterly task depending upon the efficiency of your system. Clean them more often if they are visibly contaminated with mold, pests, or vermin (and their droppings), or are clogged with substantial deposits of dust or debris.

Skin cancer outcome

Tara continues:

Adam and I went in for our biopsy appointments and there was good news and bad news. The good news was that the mark on my son's head was not in fact a cancerous lesion, but mine revealed a basal cell carcinoma, which is the most common type of skin cancer and one that can easily be taken care of. The verdict however, was that it was caused by pollutants in the environment. Just think, every time Adam and I took a walk near a major road, our skins were absorbing the toxins. So, we're moving farther into the country!

So what does this mean for my family or our planet as a whole? Such environmental toxicity becomes magnified in its ability to influence our lives when we fail to take care of our inner worlds. As my experience revealed, I have been a health conscious individual and parent for many years and believed I was making the right choices for my family. However, I had no idea what affect my outer environment was having on my physical body.

To make this story more alarming, I live at the base of the Blue Ridge Mountains, far away from a city dwelling or high traffic environment. We live beside a marginally busy road and take walks on a daily basis where breathing in the air of the vehicles has had enough impact to change the direction of our lifestyle choices. Either way, the polluted environment is affecting our physical health and having an even greater impact on our children and their future. This example demonstrates:

- The need to pay attention to our intuition about things we may discover on our kid's bodies as with the mark on Adam's head or the mark on my arm.
- An increased awareness about the types of foods and products we are using in our households and feeding our children.
- Increase the foods or vitamins you give your family to include diets rich in polyphenols.
- Be aware of environmental pollutions and focus on balancing your inner world with an awareness of the affect the outer world has on your physical body.

A child's intuition knows

We have followed Tara's intuitive nudges both with regard to her family and herself. Now Tara shares how her oldest son Adam, became intuitively aware of his own needs without being reminded.

Tara shares: "When I took the boys in for their annual physicals, I asked our doctor, a holistic health practitioner, to give the kids the sugar talk. He happily obliged, and by the time we left his office my kids thought they would never have normal food again. I reassured them I was not going to take all things out of their diet, but I *was* going to remove any products that contained high-fructose corn syrup. You would be surprised at the items that contain this one ingredient: ketchup, jellies, most BBQ sauces, and salad dressings, to name a few. I found adequate replacements for each of these items so we didn't feel restricted or deprived.

"Shortly after the changes to our diet, we moved. During the move, a friend of Adam's asked if he could have a Sprite. His mom said it was okay, so Adam asked if he could have one too. I said "sure," as I am not about to be so restrictive that he feels the need to sneak or hoard items. He took a few sips and handed the Sprite to his dad. We were shocked when he revealed the sprite was giving him a headache and he didn't want it."

Making simple changes can have a great impact on the lifestyle choices your children begin to make for themselves. If they have the ability to experience the affect and recognize the cause of it, they will be more likely to choose things that make them feel good and eliminate things that are harmful to their bodies.

Chapter Review

As much as we'd like to, we cannot wrap our children in bubble wrap and insulate them from every existing hazard in the world. Although all children are exposed to environmental toxicity, the children with sensitive immune systems and nervous systems need you to advocate and act on their behalf.

We do everything within our power to keep our children and their environment safe, starting within our own homes. From introducing an organic diet, to improving the indoor air quality of our home; from switching to natural cleaning products and integrating organic gardening methods instead of relying on pesticides are just a few measures that are simple to introduce. By taking action and implementing measures to lower environmental toxicity in our children's main environment, they are better able to read their physical needs, and become empowered to listen to and respect their health needs. We help them become better able to combat the numerous other toxins over which we as parents have no control. With a few easy lifestyle adjustments, you can bestow on your child the gift of environmental health.

The next chapter reveals provocative information that you may have read in magazines and seen in e-zines. We hope the following chapter on our children's food will empower a proactive choice to healthy diet and lifestyle as an intuitive parent for your family.

9

Intuitives at Risk: Fed Up With Food Additives

Take care of your body. It's the only place you have to live. Eat intuitively!

Children, especially the emotionally sensitive and empathic, are far more susceptible to environmental toxins than adults are for a variety of reasons, including differential intake capacities, behavioral patterns, and different absorption, metabolism, and excretion levels than adults.[1]

All of these factors combine to markedly increase the impact of environmental toxicity levels of children. Although most people might consider children to be miniature adults, physiologically this is far from the case. Consider this:

- Children ages 1 through 5 eat three to four times more per unit of body weight than the average adult.

- Infants and children drink more than 2 1/2 times as much water daily as adults on a percentage-of-body-weight basis.

- A resting infant's air intake is twice that of an adult, and a baby's surface-to-volume ratio of skin to weight is 2 1/2 times greater per unit of body mass compared to that of an adult.[2]

All of these physiological differences mean that children are exposed to environmental toxins at levels far greater than that of adults. Metabolic and excretory capacities also come into play, and those of children are much different as well, as are their pathways for chemical and toxic absorption. The kidneys are the body's principal pathways for eliminating most chemicals from the body, and an infant's kidney-filtration rate is only a fraction of that of an adult's. Many other organs are not fully mature at birth, but continue to develop during a child's formative years up through adolescence. These include (but are certainly not limited to) systems such as the sex organs, the alveoli (air sacs) of the lungs, and myelination (the insulating component of nerve fibers).[3]

A report by the Natural Resources Defense Council identifies what are known to be the worst environmental threats to children and touches on other toxins that children are routinely exposed to, either after birth or in utero. These risks include:

Lead and other heavy metals—*The U.S. Centers for Disease Control (CDC) considers lead poisoning to be the foremost environmental threat to children today. Although great strides have been made through regulatory measures (such as removing lead from paint and gasoline), the majority of lead exposure comes from eating food or drinking water that contains lead, or spending time in an environment (such as playgrounds and schools near industrial areas) where lead occurs.*

Air pollution *is rampant throughout the industrialized world, and a risk to children in both urban and rural settings. In 2004, U.S. facilities released figures indicating that more than 96 million pounds of emissions were released into the air and water. These emissions have been linked to developmental problems such as birth defects, learning disabilities, asthma, and reproductive disorders.*

Indoor air pollution *is among the top five environmental risks to public health, and levels of indoor air pollutants may be 2 to 5 (and sometimes as much as 100 times) higher than outdoor levels. They further estimated that 85 percent of the total daily exposure to airborne pesticides comes from breathing air inside the home. This pollution is not only residual from outdoor air pollutants that make their way into our homes, but also comes from chemicals and common household cleaners. Most products used in homes contain either organophosphates or carbamate pesticides, both of which are acute nervous system toxins.*

Pesticides *exposures (in both food and drinking water) serve as endocrine disruptors that can both negatively impact childhood development as well as endocrine function. They do this by disrupting the functionality of estrogen and other signaling-compounds such as thyroid hormone.*

Food additives, hyperactivity, and attention issues

Should parents take more concern for what substances are in their children's food particularly what are commonly referred to as food additives? This concern is of special importance for sensitive children.

Given the growing concern regarding obesity among children in the United States, it is quite clear that both restaurants and food companies have had little concern for the amount of high glycemic and chemical substances in our children's food. Despite the concern by certain food manufacturers emphasizing more whole grains in their cereals, it is quite true that children's cereals, in general, and other foods developed for children, are still loaded with white sugar, white flour, and other undesirable substances such as high-fructose corn syrup. This is only the tip of the iceberg with regard to chemical food additives.

Why is that?

By adding addictive substances such as refined sugars and high-fructose corn syrup that cause sharp glycemic spikes, food manufacturers are providing added neurological enjoyment to the unwary consumer, which also include children. This is analogous to enhancing the nicotine effect in cigarettes. The widespread use of sugar, sugar-like substances, and other food chemicals compounds produces addictive effects and encourages a return to these less-than-natural products. Unfortunately, young children and sensitive people are jumpstarted on this addictive cycle at an early age, particularly by bonding them early to sugary cereals and fruity juices disguised as natural and healthy.

Further, by adding artificial color, artificial flavor, and texture modifiers, corporations simply make their food look and taste more attractive. Besides creating addictive food behaviors and reinforcing branding techniques to court consumers to return to their products, there are economic reasons that food-producing corporations worldwide have an ongoing love affair with chemical preservatives and other additives. The presences of certain additives extend the shelf life of food substances, eliminate waste, and increase the sales of their products.

High glycemic substances, chemicals, and preservatives make corporations millions of dollars annually, all at a physical, emotional, psychological, and financial cost to consumers. Overall, chemicals and other food additives are used to color food, flavor food, sweeten, change, cover up smells, emulsify, bleach, disguise its bad taste, give food artificial texture, preserve, and stabilize it. As consumers, we hardly give chemical food additives a second thought. But should we?

Abundant quantity of chemicals

Before we examine the possible effects of these substances on our children, it is startling to examine the quantity of chemical substances, which are regularly added to our food supply.

As Frances M. Lappé says in *Diet for a Small Planet*, "Would you choose to sprinkle 1/4 ounce of pesticides over your food every day? Or ingest 150 pounds of assorted additives annually?" Of course not.

It is difficult to assess the pervasiveness of food additives in the United States food supply. In one officious example, the database maintained by the Food and Drug Administration and the Center for Food Safety and Applied Nutrition (CFSAN) in a program known as the Priority-based Assessment of Food (PAFA) lists information regarding more than 3,000 food additives, which includes classifications of direct, secondary "direct," color additives, and Generally Recognized as Safe (GRAS). The total list is referred to as the Everything Added to Food in the United States (EUFUS). It is in the GRAS area that a great deal of subterfuge takes place because these additives, regarded as "safe," are not listed as separate ingredients on our food labels.

Their chemical contents, surprisingly large in number, are compressed and buried under the label of artificial flavoring, color, or preservative. These are not necessarily listed in detail on the majority of food packaging. Given the potential for adverse reactions, they are the secret scourge of the food supply, and as we shall see, a particular health risk for children suffering from compromises such as autism and hyperactivity.

Paul Chek, a famous fitness trainer, is highly concerned about the effects of food products and their chemical additive contents. His concern for the health of his clients points out that the numbers cited above are just an unrealistic and low estimate. In his book, *How to Eat, Move and Be Healthy*, he says, "Including chemicals used in food production from ground to stomach, the number rises to between 10,000 and 15,000 food additives regularly ingested by the American public."

Several studies have examined various combinations of food chemicals commonly found in processed food items worldwide. The studies suggest that after the consumption of typical snack and drink items common to westernized cultures, the additives affected the nerve cells ability for normal growth and interfered with proper neurological signaling.

This is alarming for small children as their delicate systems are such that the liver is unable to fully detoxify at such a young age and their small size provokes further and compounded toxicity. Because children are small, they are consuming larger amounts of food additives than what most governments dictate as the Acceptable Daily Intake (ADI), which is based on adult consumption.

Let examine two of these studies.

A study performed by Britain's Karen Lau and her associates discovered the potentially disturbing consequences to developing brain cells when interacting with combinations involving two common food flavor enhancers with two food colorings. The first food coloring was "Brilliant Blue," used in the United States but banned by many European countries. The second, "Quinoline Yellow" is banned in Australia, Norway, and the United States, but is legal in many other countries. Aspartame, a common artificial sweetener and food flavoring is made from aspartic acid, phenylalanine, and methanol. Finally, also MSG, an acronym for L-glutamic acid commonly used in the USA and Europe. Lau then made two "cocktails" of MSG mixed with Brilliant Blue and aspartame with Quinoline Yellow, which were tested on mouse neuroblastoma cells, used as the prototype for neurons.

First testing these substances individually, the researchers found that Brilliant Blue inhibited neural growth the most, followed in order by MSG, Quinoline Yellow, and aspartame. But mixed together in their cocktail combinations, the capacity for neural inhibition was much larger for the mixtures than their individual effects on the neuroblastoma cells. Lau's colleagues stated, "The results indicate that certain combinations are potentially more toxic than might be predicted from the sum of their individual compounds."

In fact, the MSG/Brilliant Blue presented four times the neuro toxicity as the sum of the individual substances and the aspartame/Quinoline Yellow was up to seven times as toxic in its effects.

Following these findings, the researchers analyzed the contents of five British snacks and drinks and looked at the effect on a 22-pound child. They found that one snack and drink, containing these mixtures, could theoretically cause nerve growth inhibition. This is a startling commentary on the poignancy of common substances to affect nerve cells. Consuming these substances, the researchers said, could have long-term neurological consequences.

According to the editorial comments from the Autism Research Institute on the summary of this experiment from which this account is derived, "This report provides yet more evidence supporting the theory that autism and related disabilities involve 'excitotoxins' such as MSG and aspartame—and more proof that junk food, laced with preservatives, artificial sweeteners, and colorings, is a major culprit in the current epidemic of learning and behavioral disorders." The concerns of the Autism community, in this comment, transcends merely the speculation about food additive affects on autism, per se, but also for other neurogenic disorders, which include hyperactivity, of which ADD is the most well-known.

A breakthrough study at the University of Southampton, led by Jim Stevenson, a professor of psychology, has confirmed that certain food additives are a cause of hyperactivity in children. According to Elizabeth Rosenthal, a *New York Times* reporter, "It was the first time researchers conclusively and scientifically confirmed a link that had long been suspected by many parents. Numerous support groups for attention deficit hyperactivity disorder have for years recommended removing such ingredients from diets, although experts have continued to debate the evidence."

Researchers in the report said, "A mix of additives commonly found in children's foods increases the mean level of hyperactivity.... The finding lends strong support for the case that food additives exacerbate hyperactive behaviors (inattention, impulsivity and over activity) at least into middle childhood."

Proof that chemicals affect brain and behavior

As hyperactivity is a common symptom experienced by autistic children, this finding could explain the beneficial effects achieved by autistic patients when ingesting diets formulated without food additives. But the affect on autistic children is probably a relatively small subset when compared to the prevalence of children with ADD and other hyperactive and developmental disorders. All in all, tens of thousands of children have had their own unique body balance upset by these toxic substances.

Unlike the previous study we have cited, this study directly involved the behavior of children, whose behavior was closely monitored during a six-week period. The children's reactions were to several food colors and to sodium benzoate, a preservative. These children were given these additives in doses simulating those found in commercially marketed substances. The dosages were comparable to one or two portions of candy daily. The sample consisted of a randomly selected group of several hundred 8- to 9-year-olds and 3-year-olds. These substances were provided to the children in an overall meal regimen meant to avoid contamination of their intake by any other food additives or preservatives that could offset the purity of the experimental conditions. At the same time this group was being fed sodium benzoate combined with other food additives, another random group of the same size was fed a placebo of the same size and color.

A group of parents and teachers of school age children, unaware of who had actually taken the real drink or the placebo, then monitored the behavior of these children. Findings were established through a direct study of their hyperactivity, inattention, and by a computer test.

The results were startling. After consuming the experimental drink, children became more hyperactive with much shorter attention spans. This happened approximately one hour after drinking. The study showed statistically significant changes to the behavior of the selected group, but it could not determine the affect of the specific additives. Suffice to say, the cocktail did create hyperactivity and loss of attention, but future studies would be necessary to determine specific causes of behavior and their link to the specific substances used.

Research into the field of testing food additives will probably blossom in further years, but decades after manufacturers and other contributors to the food chain have already contaminated our food supply.

Common food additives

1. Allura Red AC (E129): An orange-red food dye used in foods, beverages, pharmaceuticals, cosmetics, and some tattoo inks. It is a synthetic azo dye that replaced Amaranth E123 in the United States. It is not recommended for children in Europe and is banned in some countries. Results of a UK study found that a mixture of preservatives that included allura red AC E129 resulted in heightened hyperactivity in children.

2. Aspartame: This is a well-documented neurotoxin and excitotoxin that has well-documented and direct adverse effects on brain function. Aspartame accounts for the majority of adverse reaction complaints reported to the FDA. Aspartame is a widely used artificial sweetener.

3. Brilliant Blue Food Dye: This is a food dye used to raise appeal of foods and beverages such as condiments, candies, syrups, dairy products, icings, jellies, extracts, and powders. A study published in *The Lancet*, a medical journal, revealed hyperactivity in children due to artificial food dyes. Dyes have also been linked to migraines, reflux, asthma, and some rashes.

4. Butylparaben: This is a derivative of a diverse and widely used family of chemicals used as a food preservative. The families of parabens are used as antibacterial and antifungal agents in food, cosmetics, and medications. Synthetically produced, derivatives of the paraben chemical group can be found in use worldwide.

5. Disodium Insonate: This chemical compound is used as a flavor enhancer in potato chips and flavored noodles. It often occurs with monosodium glutimate.

6. High-Fructose Corn Syrup: This is a form of sugar derived from cornstarch called fructose. It is sweeter than sugar and also less expensive. It is used extensively in processed foods as a sweetener and also a preservative. It is associated with elevated LDL

cholesterol and triglyceride levels, insulin insensitivity, and weight gain.

7. Natamycin: This is an anti-fungal agent produced by fermenting the bacteria Streptomyces natalynsis. This bacterium is commonly found in soil. As a drug, it is used to treat Fusarium corneal infections and fungal keratitis. Natamycin is used to stop fungal growth in meats and dairy products to include yogurt, cheese, and sour cream.

8. Polydi Methylsiloxane: (PDMS): This is a silicon-based polymer with applications in the production of silicone caulks, adhesives, lubricants, polishes, and cosmetics. PDMS is used in the treatment of head lice. Its application in food production is that of an anti-foaming and anti-caking agent and is widely used by the fast food industry.

9. Quinoline Yellow (E104): Food dye with a yellow or green-yellow color. This is found in squash, OTC tablets, smoked fish, pickles, and some sweets—also a tattoo ink color. It is associated with hyperactivity and certain rashes, and could be a cause of contact dermatitis. Usage is not allowed in the United States or Japan, but is permitted in the UK.

10. Sodium Nitrate: This chemical compound is used in the curing of meat in order to prevent bacterial growth and also gives meats their rich dark red color. Sodium nitrite is a well-documented toxin and is lethal in larger doses. August 2008 brings the U.S. based news of a meat packing plant employee who gave her neighbor sodium nitrite capsules; just enough to hospitalize the neighbor, but not a large enough dose to kill her. The point: the employee of the meat packing plant was familiar with the potential toxicity of sodium nitrite and used her knowledge to her advantage to cause harm to another.

11. Reduced Iron: This chemical compound is produced by the reduction of iron ore via a reduction gas such as natural gas. The end result is a metallic iron. The oxidation state during this process provides the "nutritional iron" found in processed food items. Reduced iron has industrial applications in the steel industry.

12. Modified Cornstarch: This is corn flour, which is used as thickener in processed foods and as talc in baby powder. Corn allergies are rampant in pediatric populations.

13. Monosodium Glutamate: A flavoring agent. It is a sodium salt of an amino acid called glutamic acid. It is made by fermentation with products such as molasses and food starch from cereal grains or tapioca. The FDA has classified MSG a food additive that is "generally recognized as safe" however, the while recognizing that some individuals have short-term adverse reactions to MSG. The FDA requires MSG to be listed on food ingredient labels and on restaurant menus when used.

14. Sodium Benzoate Preservative: It is bacteria static and fungi static in acidic products such as soft drinks, condiments, salad dressings, pickles, juices, jams, squash, cough syrups, and mouthwash. Research by the South Hampton University study for the Food Standards Agency found that along with other additives, this preservative was found to affect behavior problems and affect intelligence in children. According to claims from a professor at University of Sheffield, Sodium benzoate may have an adverse affect on DNA, which may play a part in neurodegenerative diseases such as Parkinson's, plus help accelerate the overall aging process.

15. Sunset Yellow (E110) V Food Dye: An orange-yellow color used widely in drinks, sweets, and other foods. Included as one out of six artificial colorings, in the study for the FSA in September 2007, that may induce hyperactivity in children.

16. Tartrazine (E102) Food Dye: Synthetic lemon yellow dye from coal tar and found in snacks, drinks, powders, and condiments. Found to cause hyperactivity in children when mixed with several other food additives and certain preservatives.

Toxins accumulate through time

The fact that chemical additives cause problems related to neural transmission is further enhanced with the understanding that certain mixtures of various additives significantly increase the possible effect on a child's state of hyperactivity. The full extent of this phenomenon leaves much to be examined scientifically because most additives occur in mixtures when consumed in food products. With the science largely unknown, do we have time bombs hidden in our refrigerators and pantry shelves that have caused and will cause increasing damage to our children?

A review published in the February 2008 edition of the *AAP Grand Rounds*, a publication of the American Academy of Pediatrics, contains a profound statement by Alison Schonwald, MD, FAAP, cited as an expert in developmental and behavioral pediatrics at Children's Hospital in Boston.

"A recent meta-analysis of 15 trials concludes that there is "accumulating evidence that neurobehavioral toxicity may characterize a variety of widely distributed chemicals…. Some children may be more sensitive to the effects of these chemicals, and the authors suggest there is a need to better identify responders. For the child without a medical, emotional, or environmental etiology of ADHD behaviors, a trial of a preservative-free, food coloring–free diet is a reasonable intervention."[4]

Jane Hersey, the director of the non-profit Feingold Association, an organization that directly encourages the use of a preservative-free, food coloring-free diet, recently wrote about the link between hyperactivity and children in a feature article in the November/December 2007 journal about how school behavior changes when diet changes. She cited a study of what happened "when 803 New York City public schools eliminated certain artificial colors, flavors, and preservatives from their breakfast and lunch programs."

This four-year study conducted by Stephen J. Schjoenthaler under the auspices of California State University showed a dramatic shift from scores on the California Achievement Test from the 55th to the 39th percentile. This was an upward shift of almost 16 percent. Almost 75,000 children, who had been considered learning disabled or very low achievers, were now able to perform at their age level, with the only difference being some dietary changes," said Hersey.

Again, although everyone needs to avoid food chemicals at all costs, our children's sensitive neurological systems are at stake. Quite disturbing is the issue of the combinations of food additives that have been explored in the recent studies we have just examined. How these agents react together is fueling further concerns as to the continued neurotoxic effects on our nation's children. It appears that certain combinations of chemical food additives have a potent and negative effect on nerve cells than each chemical would have if ingested alone.

Although everyone needs to reduce or eliminate their exposure to food chemicals, this is particularly true with regards to children suffering the symptoms of some form of autism (Autism Spectrum Disorder or ASD), ADHD, and other developmental delays. This is the group that seemingly is more sensitive to food chemicals than others. Unfortunately, of all populations, it is predominantly children that will have immediate reactions upon the ingestion of processed foods laden with artificial substances. Although artificial colors and sweeteners have proven particularly problematic for children, it would be safe to surmise that all food chemicals should be avoided; in particular where young children are already experiencing neurological challenges.

Perhaps an examination of some of the diets, such as the Feingold diet, the Body Ecology Diet, the Specific Carbohydrate diet, and the Gluten Free diet might produce some beneficial paradigms for intuitive, sensitive children. Whatever diet is labeled or pursued, a fresh whole food, organic diet without chemicals, preservatives, food colors, food flavors, and pesticide residues removed, is undoubtedly the safest, most conservative food route to pursue, given both the anecdotal and scientific findings of today.

Chapter Review

Children, especially the emotionally sensitive and empathic, are far more susceptible to environmental toxins than adults.

Children are exposed to environmental toxins at levels far greater than that of adults. Metabolic and excretory capacities also come into play, and those of children are much different as well, as are their pathways for chemical and toxic absorption.

Nurturing the Creative Intuitive

The creation of something new is not accomplished by the intellect but by the play instinct acting from inner necessity. The creative mind plays with the objects it loves.

—Carl Jung

Creative-intuitive

In earlier chapters, we presented the model of natural intelligences common to all people: physical, mental-creative, emotional-social, intuitive, and spiritual. These intelligences reveal the whole person. When intelligence is paired with the strength of intuition, a uniquely gifted person emerges and their environments nurture and shape their expressions.

In this chapter, we focus on the creative intuitive, a child whose strongest intelligences are mental-creative and intuitive as shown in the following chart. Creativity is a capacity of every learner, as is intuition, and deserves exploration and opportunity for expression. We want all children to explore dance, painting, drama, music, and other artistic pursuits as part of their life experience.

Natural Intelligences	Plus Intuitive Intelligence =
Physical Prowess Enhanced by Intuitive Intelligence	
Physical	*Learns by doing, has exceptional kinesthesia, motor skills, sense of timing, and movement with the body.*
Creative, Inspired Intuitive	
Mental-Creative	*Inspired, inventive, creative, follows inner music, ideas, and actions motivated by internal genius. Can daydream, be distracted, learns to focus, and learns through experimentation.*
Empathic Intuitive	
Emotional-Social	*Reads others, feels others, defines self in relation to others. Needs boundaries, emotional management skills, self-identification, and confidence.*
Psychic Intuitive	
Intuitive	*Expanded awareness of the nonphysical worlds or subtle energy fields through receptors in the biochemistry. Exhibits talents of subtle knowing, hearing, seeing, telepathy, and other talents.*
Spiritual Intuitive	
Spiritual	*Intuition serves kids with spiritual intelligence as the doorway and interpreter to connection with inner worlds.*

Creative intelligence is more than a growing interest in a talent. Bruce Hammonds, an educational advisor in New Zealand, helps schools transform their learning communities. He says, "True creativity requires rigor, courage, personal effort and a sense of personal quality. Creative results do often come easily to learners but more often requires complex reasoning processes...."[1]

Characteristics of the creative-intuitive

The type of creative intelligence that a child has emerges early, sometimes in their preschool years, and this is when their grasp of a topic involves intuition. Watching three preschool boys in a playroom with trucks brought insight. Eric put the trucks in an upside down position and turned the wheels round and round, mesmerized by their movement. Brad took the trucks and pretended that the tables were highways. He lined the trucks along the table edge and created his own truck path. Jason took the little people out of the driver's seats, detached other pieces where he could and asked how one truck was made. Can you see the future engineer, racecar or truck driver, and architect?

Each boy's natural intuition guided his interests and curiosity. Some specific aspect of the trucks made sense to each boy. We can see where, how, and to what our child is drawn to explore and observe through play. Then we nurture a child's intuitive intelligence for positive learning experiences. For example, being an intuitive athlete is a different gift than that of the intuitive linguist who creates lyrical poems or from the intuitive mathematician who grasps calculus. In *The Exceptional Mind*, author Dr. Robert Flower suggests that intuition in an exceptional thinking skill, which is unique to each child's natural learning style.

Because the creative intuitives learn through exploration and hands-on experiences, they need to approach their tasks in their own way. As a teen, Linda had the craziest wish to learn to sew. This was not unusual for Linda. Her mom had seen Linda's passion to learn a new task rise quickly in her childhood. She took Linda's lead and taught her how to make simple shifts and loose yoga pants. Then Linda hit a glitch when her brain could not discern the correct way to sew in a zipper. After several sessions with no success, Linda became upset and her mother backed away because she knew that Linda could tackle a task with no background knowledge and figure it out. Linda displayed amazing tenacity. Linda taught herself to sew the zipper in upside down and backwards, and it worked. Linda's sister commented a dozen times that it was wrong, to redo it. Linda put on her pants, zipped them up, and went to her yoga class. Linda had to feel her way through the process, and she succeeded.

Other traits that characterize creative-intuitive style

They are willing to think outside the box or have innovative ideas. For example, Kenneth loved to write, but the small, private school he attended had no courses on literature or creative writing. Yet Kenneth's passion was not ignored. He found other students who wanted to write and they formed a club. The club members raised money to print a quarterly review of their work.

Their approaches are original, whether in seeing a problem or presenting a solution. They can find the resources in their innocence or naiveté to make magic. A Website called *www.DinosaurTales.com* invites young writers to showcase their stories. At age 14 Zachary Ebers collected thousands of boxes of cereal for children to have breakfast throughout the summer because they had previously relied on free school breakfasts for their meal.[2]

They are inspired by their inner flow of thoughts, music, daydreams, or inspirations. Tom, not encumbered by books and learning, heard music in his head most every weekend when his family took him to the Maryland shores. As his parents played bridge and socialized, Tom collected shark's teeth and hummed the tunes he heard inside, yet he could not read music nor play a note. As an adult, he created CDs of his music with the help of a musician.

They have active imaginations. Every summer, Eloise went with her family to their cabin in the White Mountains of New Hampshire. To Eloise, each rock gave voice to the many people who climbed them. Smaller rocks became wheels and circles in the field. Tiny stones were privileges to form piles and mark trails through the woods.

They can see the world through an artist's eye, a musician's ear, an inventor's innovation, and need the room and ability to express. Rules, classrooms, agendas—all such ties that set boundaries for creatives—can feel suffocating.

Hardwired for creative-intuition

Emma Policastro answered the question if creative intuition exits. She authored a review of evidence for creative intuition founded upon her four research bases:

1. Historical evidence.
2. Autobiographies.
3. Psychometric assessments.
4. Experimental studies.

Policastro concedes that the "notion of creative intuition is coherent, well grounded, and empirically testable."[3] Creative mental intelligence and intuitive intelligence are synergistic.

In the literal sense, a creative mind sees the world differently than other minds. This state of seeing innovatively is induced by new experiences. Novel experiences spark the creative biochemistry, and intuitive intelligence provides the doorway to novelty: listening to the gut brain, exploring feelings using interpretive drama. The popularity of the book, *The Artist's Way* (Tarcher/ Putnam, 2002), broke people's perception of reality and taught them to see a new way. Painting, for instance, opens the right brain to expressing its capability. Intuition steers the motivation and forms the pattern for learning.

The same brain circuits are used for perception and imagination. Novel experiences unleash the imagination because they force the brain to take shortcuts, reorganize, and see differently. The harder we try to think of something different and creative, the more confined the brain pattern becomes.[4] In short, creative and inspiring ideas happen when the mind cannot predict the same previous patterns. The more radical the novel experience, the deeper the insight. The perceptual system is forced to reorganize its circuits.

Critical role of imagination

Imagination is a potent ingredient for our children's creative intuition—one that serves as the foundation for a host of needed life skills.

Self-dialog is a component of imaginative play that helps children learn to overcome obstacles and master the art of self-regulation. Unstructured imaginative play also serves to round out a child's whole-person development.

Recent studies show that imaginative play has changed drastically in the past 60 years, and that children's development is suffering because of it. One study conducted in 2001 intended to compare results to a similar study from the late 1940s. Its goal was to test children's capacity for self-regulation.

In the 1940s study, the researchers tested children ages 3, 5, and 7 by asking them to stand perfectly still without moving. The 3-year-olds could not stand still at all, the 5-year-olds could for about three minutes, and most of the 7-year-olds could stand still for as long as the researchers asked.

Compare this to the astonishing results from the 2001 study at the Mid-Continent Research for Education and Learning. The 5-year-olds could only stand upright for a length of time previously measured in 3-year-olds. More tellingly, the 7-year-olds of today were barely approaching the level of 5-year-olds from more than a half-century ago.

Why is imaginative play such a critical component in developing self-regulation? During periods of make-believe and pretend, children engage in self-dialog—a life skill that empowers them to learn to overcome obstacles, master cognitive and social skills, and manage their emotions. Using self-talk regulates the intuitive driver to explore and learn.

During this period of self-dialog, or private speech, children decide on desired objectives and then strategize ways to accomplish those feats. Self-dialog is also a tool that adults still utilize when faced with challenges or problems. By talking things through, we're able to process situations, analyze them, and design solutions for them.

Studies also show that creative and imaginative play can aid in five other areas of development:

1. Memory.
2. Attitude.
3. Planning.
4. Attention.
5. Creativity.

Imaginative play also helps children expand and hone their language and communication skills.

Many scientists are concerned about the shift in culture. Until television sets were introduced into mainstream lives, childhood play revolved around some type of activity rather than today's usual object-centric type of play.

Before television, children used everyday objects to create scenarios and to imagine a world of their own. A stick in a boy's hand had the capacity to become a knight's sword, a fishing pole, or a Native American spear. Today's product commercialization has removed the realm of limitless possibilities, and now tends to pigeonhole children into a pre-conceived situation, such as Luke Skywalker's lightsaber, where the intent of the object is already clear and denies the child a chance to find a creative purpose for the object.

Another area of concern is the loss of unstructured time that allows children to engage in imaginative play. From soccer and baseball games to piano and karate lessons, children today have far less time than past generations to let their imaginations run free. Leagues and lessons offer many benefits to children. Yet, when kids are engaged in structured activities, they are not learning to manage themselves. Instead the adults in their lives are regulating them. Scientists have noted that the more structured the play, the more children's private speech and self-dialog decline. Structuring a child's free time leaves them with less available for imaginative play when they learn to self-regulate.

Compound this with the overwhelming numbers of electronic devices that serve not to expand children's minds, but to numb them, and you can easily understand why our kids have fallen behind in their abilities to become self-sufficient.

Why is self-regulation such an important life skill? Studies have shown that good self-regulation skills are a better predictor of success in school and life than a child's IQ. Children are able to control their own behavior, manage their feelings, and keep themselves on task—all elements that contribute to high creative intelligence, intuition, and success.

What are some ways you as a parent can encourage imaginative play in your child? Here are just a few to get you started:

- Limit television viewing and time spent playing computer or electronic games.
- Schedule time for imaginative play, just as you would schedule time for piano lessons or soccer practice.
- Encourage interaction between peers by letting your child have friends over or go to a friend's house.

Peer interaction often drives the imaginative process, and develops children's social, language, and problem-solving abilities.

Although play dates may be popular, make sure that you or other parents allow children to interact together at their own level and pace, rather than dictating for them how the play date unfolds.

Parents can also interact with children in a variety of ways that let children master creativity through imagination. These include:

Creating stories together, where you each take turns adding a thread to the tale. You can start the process by finding an everyday object and verbalizing a sentence or two about it to create a scenario. Then, let your child take over and embellish the tale from there. As you go back and forth adding to the story, you'll stimulate and challenge both of your imaginations.

Provide tools for make believe. Have objects such as pots and pans with spoons, and building blocks and craft supplies on hand that you keep in the "Imagination Drawer." Then, make sure to direct your child to the magic drawer when she says, "I'm bored."

Play the "Imagine If" game. Whether you're in your garden or driving along in the car, look for objects and then start conversations with, "Imagine if …"—that is, "Imagine if roses were blue," or "Imagine if birds swam and fish flew." This helps children hone their visual processing and cognitive skills, and opening them up to seeing the world in new ways.

Just as exercise is important to the physical muscles, imaginative play allows children to build their creative and problem-solving "muscles." By making sure to incorporate imaginative play in our children's lives, we give them the capacity to become self-regulated problem-solvers—ones whose futures are limited only by their boundless imagination.

Disordered, distracted, or dreamers?

"Indeed, while many experts automatically link overexcited, impulsive, and even disruptive behavior to ADHD, there are some who believe this same conduct may simply be the earmarks of profound creativity looking for a way to flourish."[5]

When creative, intuitive children are distracted, most of the time creativity is flowing and they are focused on their internal rhythms, words, or projects. They may be distracted, but it doesn't mean they are disordered. Especially for an observant, ingenious, or inventive child, handling their fast-flowing thoughts and rushes of feelings may not happen until they learn and practice management skills such as focusing and shifting moods. Daydreamers are paying attention, but often to their inner worlds. We need to help them manage it, so that they can be aware of what's going on inside their feelings and daydreams and respond to their environment.

Being creative doesn't mean a free spirit or a disordered mind. The medical model, which searches for symptoms to quash, tries to fit into an educational system where children of different temperaments, learning styles, and strengths struggle to learn and fit in the box. Are we there yet?

The creative intuitive can be expected to have great ideas, and may or may not have the skills to get the idea in form and finished. This is where we come in to provide resources, modeling, demonstration, and support. "If you give these kids creative ways to expend a day's worth of pent-up energy, they will remain more engaged and interested in all things, and with or without ADHD their creativity will flourish," says Bonnie Cramond, director of Torrance Center for Creative Study, University of Georgia, Athens.[6]

The intuitive focus of creative minds while they are "in the zone" causes us to respond kindly, without loud disruption, and remind them to take care of themselves. The creative mind engages reverie and imaginal worlds just as effortlessly as the intuitive empath mirrors people's feelings.

The creative intuitive is an explorer of worlds unknown to most people, that of the "depth-self" and the "authentic self." The intuitive creative displays six important traits:

1. Self-sufficient.
2. Independent.
3. Persistent.
4. Pioneering.
5. Influential.
6. Openness to their inner world.

Creating an enriched environment

- Turn off the television. Creative children are observant and need the time to be in stillness.
- Practice creative movement. Dance to different kinds of music; demonstrate positive emotions with hands, arms, and body postures.
- At least twice a month, get out of the house and visit museums, nature parks, and tours of interesting places. Explore the local library and stimulate novelty.
- Showing the value of focus and knowledge by researching an answer together.
- Decorate with stimulating, primary colors, which are creative.
- Design a creative wall for doodles by using chalkboard paint and washable markers.
- Reuse in craft projects the usual throwaways such as egg cartons, paper rolls, fabrics, plastics, and wrapping paper.

Chapter Review

- The type of creative intelligence that a child has emerges early, sometimes in their preschool years, and this is when their grasp of a topic involves intuition.

- Policastro concedes that the "notion of creative intuition is coherent, well grounded, and empirically testable."[7] Creative mental intelligence and intuitive intelligence are synergistic.

- In the literal sense, a creative mind sees the world differently than other minds. This state of seeing innovatively is induced by new experiences.

- Novel experiences spark the creative biochemistry.

- Imagination is a potent ingredient for our children's creative intuition—one that serves as the foundation for a host of needed life skills.

- Self-dialog is a component of imaginative play that helps children learn to overcome obstacles and master the art of self-regulation.

11

Emotional Support for Empathic Intuitives

What I am actually saying is that we need to be willing to let our intuition guide us, and then be willing to follow that guidance directly and fearlessly.
—Shakti Gawain, motivational speaker and author

We mentioned in previous chapters that intuitive children, whether creative intellectuals, empathic feelers, psychics, or inspired artists, negotiate three environments in their lives: the physical world, the non-physical world, and the spiritual world. Intuitive children who have good self-esteem, show resilience, and feel valued in their families are happy kids! This chapter addresses support for the empathic intuitive.

Empathic feelers have acute mental or emotional sensibilities, and as children want to be responsive to other people's feelings. Yet, at times, their sensitivity threshold is low. They are often told, "You are too sensitive," rather than being recognized for their gifts.

What a delight when a child is recognized for his gift of empathy! Our friend, Minette, shared that when her sensitive son Conner was 5 years old and entered kindergarten, she went to work in launching a local parenting newspaper. One week of every month was pressure-filled with newspaper deadlines, and Conner's response was to feel his mom's stress and become distressed.

He ended up getting into trouble at school for pushing another child into a locker. The teacher was clear that he was provoked, but expressed concern that Conner, a normally happy, relaxed child, should react aggressively. After a lengthy discussion about what was going on at home, Minette realized that Conner would react to her stress at work by acting out at school.

She learned to help Conner through these stressful times by giving him plenty of advance notice about the timing of her busy-ness. She would tell Conner, "I won't be home much this week" or, "You won't see me as often this week, but once we get to Saturday, I will have the whole weekend to spend with you." By managing her own stress and preparing Conner, she gave him language and a way to healthfully express his distress at not seeing her enough during that week of the month.

Experts agree that happy children share characteristics such as optimism and a sense of control. How can parents create a supportive family atmosphere to create successful intuitive children? This chapter starts with how to provide support for the emotional empath and help them develop calm and resilience. The next several chapters will show you how to provide support for intuitive children's emotionality and sensitivity.

- Our support goal for an emotional empath is to strengthen emotional energy, especially of the heart, and empower resilience so they can interact with the environment, not withdraw from it.

- Our support goal for the creative inventor is to enable focus skills so he is aware in his worlds, and translates creativity into expression.

- Our support goal for the psychic child is to enable discernment among their many worlds and for them to become fearless and accepting of what or who faces them.

Home's emotional atmosphere

This section suggests ways to monitor and maintain an emotionally healthy atmosphere in your home. An empath's vulnerability can also be their challenge in an emotionally toxic home where they may learn to cut off their feelings. The primary home environment provides the first stable space in which an intuitive child learns to value their feelings and how to interpret the emotional atmosphere of the home. Margaret's story shows how a psychic child can interpret a parent's emotions through her clairvoyance. Her decision as a child affected her relationship with her father significantly.

Margaret's intuitive gift was emotional empathy, and she came from a large Italian family of seven children. All were talkative and emotionally expressive. Her family had a celebration for Margaret's First Communion day and invited relatives and members of the church community. It was normal to see the men in her family drinking beer and sometimes wine at these family celebrations. In the late afternoon, Margaret observed her father's emotional energy for the first time: "I kept staring at Dad because I had never seen storm clouds around him before. Usually Dad was all sunshine and smiles. I was seeing my father's aura. His alcoholic haze looked like dark clouds, and his mood was angry. Even though I was used to his booming Italian voice, when his emotional tone changed to anger, his voice matched the dark clouds seen by my young eyes. I was confused and that day was the start of my withdrawal from his energy. Being in touch with his dark storm clouds made me feel sick to my stomach. My father's alcoholism grew through the years, and our relationship withered."

Rather than Margaret withdrawing from her father to feel safe, another option would be to create communication and understanding between them—a path of resilience for Margaret. Research from The International Resilience Project reviewed what we mentioned in Chapter 1: "A child's own genetic make-up and temperament are fundamental to whether he or she will be resilient. That is, a child's vulnerability to anxiety, challenges, stress, or unfamiliarity determines his or her self-perception, how he or she interacts with others, and how he or she addresses adversities."[1]

An emotional empath like Margaret needs an adult in the family to model acceptance of other's differences. A mentor, whether a parent, sibling, neighbor, or schoolteacher can help sensitive children negotiate adversity by talking about it. For example, an adult could help Margaret clarify that her dad only looked foggy when drinking alcohol. How did his energy appear at other times? Perhaps Margaret could have brought to his attention the fact that his children did not respond well to the anger and alcohol mix. Conversations have to happen!

Among the emotional factors that contribute to negative, even toxic, emotional atmospheres in homes are:

- Surprise or intense outbursts from anger or control issues.
- Verbal putdowns or psychological bullying.
- Physical abuse, including spanking, inappropriate sexual touching, and harassment.
- Substance abuse and its vampire-like energy drain.
- Resentment, lack of respect and inappropriate behavior derived from bullying tactics such as pushing, hitting, punching, and knuckling the head.

Any child will buckle when subjected to such behaviors. The behaviors can cripple or devastate empathic or emotional intuitives who feel more profoundly. The potential for emotional harm inflicted on sensitive children has far larger ramifications than for other temperament styles. Take extra care with empathic children for health, immune system strength, and the ability to develop resilience. They must build strength to be able to stand up for themselves or know when to withdraw. All children need a champion, and empathic children need an especially caring one.

Kellie had two younger brothers, and all three children were close growing up in a single parent household. All three children remember a household of humor, movies and popcorn, long walks, and stories at bedtime during their preschool years. Kellie's mother, Leslie, remarried when Kellie was 9 years old, and her brothers were ages 8 and 7. The tenor of their household changed from happy to distressful. Their stepfather argued with Leslie, worked at night and slept during the days, and the children felt like they walked on eggshells.

One morning before school, Kellie's brothers were up to no good and broke an item in their living room. No one confessed to the crime, so Leslie put all three children in the bathroom, closed the door, and told them if one of them didn't confess, she would have their father spank all three of them.

Well, no one confessed, but empathic Kelly was a nervous wreck after waiting in the bathroom for two hours for her stepfather to come home. Her bladder was full, and when her stepfather walked through the bathroom door with a belt in his hand, she broke down and sobbed. He made each child pull down their pants, lean over his lap, and he spanked them with the belt. Kellie urinated all over him, sobbed, and was in shock.

She turned white and fell to the floor at being assaulted. When she curled into a fetal position, her brothers ran to Leslie to report that something was wrong. Kellie was put to bed where she ran a fever for three days and vomited as if she had the flu. As an adult, Kellie described her impression as seeing the evil in her stepfather and feeling vulnerable when spanked. "I felt like I swallowed his violence, absorbed it like a sponge, so intensely that I fell ill. I had to purge my body through vomiting." I had nightmares well into my teen years of being assaulted again. From that day forward, I hated the man and my mother for the way she dealt with a child's simple mistake."

Handle empathic children with care, respect, and kindness.

Restoring calm and strength

Through empathic touch, you teach an intuitive child to trust his sense of feeling and his body's messages. By pairing touch with empathy you teach the child to calm himself, a trait that every teacher who labels a child hyperactive is seeking. When a child touches his own heart, laying the palm to rest on the chest, he harmonizes his energy and synchronizes the body's rhythm. He brings chaos to comfort and distractions to center.

Holding your child next to your heart is the most effective way to feel strength. Heart-to-heart hugs look like cradling the child in your lap, his back to your chest, or kneeling down to your child's level and embracing her heart to yours. Rocking also creates a calm state for younger children. A child can also place his hand on his heart and settle into the feeling of it for several seconds to produce calm.

Tender loving touch is important throughout one's entire life, especially for the empath. In the developing embryo, a layer of cells called the ectoderm produces the skin and the nervous system. In this concrete physiological connection, touch provides "food" to the nervous system for the human to experience.

Purposeful, empathic touch to regulate and support an intuitive child's physiology tells the nervous system to be resilient and calm.

Natural Intelligences	Plus Intuitive Intelligence =
Physical Prowess Enhanced by Intuitive Intelligence	
Physical	*Learns by doing, has exceptional kinesthesia, motor skills, sense of timing, and movement with the body.*
Creative, Inspired Intuitive	
Mental-Creative	*Inspired, inventive, creative, follows inner music, ideas, and actions motivated by internal genius. Can daydream, be distracted, learns to focus, and learns through experimentation.*
Empathic Intuitive	
Emotional-Social	*Reads others, feels others, defines self in relation to others. Needs boundaries, emotional management skills, self-identification, and confidence.*
Psychic Intuitive	
Intuitive	*Expanded awareness of the nonphysical worlds or subtle energy fields through receptors in the biochemistry. Exhibits talents of subtle knowing, hearing, seeing, telepathy, and other talents.*
Spiritual Intuitive	
Spiritual	*Intuition serves kids with spiritual intelligence as the doorway and interpreter to connection with inner worlds.*

Resilience after a disconnect

At age 10, empathic Tess experienced a sudden and abrupt disconnect from her mom, which would affect her for the rest of her life. One day her mom was hugging her after school and teaching her how to cut vegetables. The next day, her Mom did not see her, but looked past her with a distant gaze and spaced-out eyes. Mom told Tess that the voices in her head told her to pull the plugs out of the walls.

Such a rapid disconnection from her mom was worse than losing her mom to death in Tess's eyes. Rather than being able to say goodbye, Tess had to renegotiate the emotional environment with her mom still alive, yet not present.

Tess was empathic. She felt as her mom felt, and had no way to talk about it or understand it. The result was that Tess withdrew, cried, and felt isolated and hurt.

Tess felt threatened by her mom's withdrawal. She also loved her Mom, so Tess split her attention in half. One half stayed hidden inside a sensitive heart, protecting and armoring. One half relearned how to live in a home with her mother's mental illness, diagnosed as Schizoid Affective Disorder. Tess was on constant psychic alert.

An intuitive cannot sustain the long-term division of attention in a situation such as Tess experienced without negative consequences. Have you ever walked forward in life while trying to watch your back every two minutes? It would distort your attention and create tension in the same way emotional intensity or trauma strike empathic children. Sensitive children will

- internalize the toxic feeling that they are the burden.
- feel inadequate or unloved and turn the messages into negative self-talk.
- feel inconsequential, like they have no power or resources in their environment.

These adversarial moments are also brilliant opportunities for developing flexibility and strength rather than being resigned. Help your children develop habits of coping so they become self-confident and trust their intuitive intelligence.

Tess's therapist had her close her eyes, relax, and go back to age 10 when she disconnected from the Mom she knew. Tess felt a giant creature standing beside her left shoulder much like a Wookiee of the Star Wars epics. This imaginary friend became Tess's protector. She could hide behind him to feel safe, and could control her world in this way. This was a resilience creation, which let Tess control her inner world when she couldn't control the outer.

Acknowledging an emotionally empathic child

Tara's younger son Caden is an emotionally empathic child. Tara can expect that potentially three to five days a week she will have to manage an emotional meltdown with Caden when he returns home from school. Because he feels the energy of everyone around him, he spends most of his day running the emotions of the other children in the classroom. By the time he gets home, he is unable or unwilling to discuss what he has been dealing with, which makes it difficult for Tara or her husband Chris to prepare for a potential meltdown.

When an emotional overload occurs, what kinds of things can parents initiate to alleviate some of the emotional stress empathic children absorb?

The most important thing parents of an emotionally empathic child can do is acknowledge their feelings regardless of how minor the incident may appear. Offering support by saying things like "I understand why you feel this way," or, "I know this situation is difficult for you. What would make you feel better so we can move on?" are helpful ways to calm the waters. All children want to be understood and respected for their feelings, but empathic children specifically need to be validated so they can focus and release. Otherwise, avoided or suppressed emotions become stored in the body, causing more stress.

Tara shares, "Caden will come home from school and seem down, even depressed. I ask him what's bothering him, but often he doesn't have a clear-cut answer. Later in the day, something will set him off and we will spend 20 minutes or so managing anger or tears to get to the bottom of the emotion. If we try to show him a different point of view he will get even more upset saying, "you aren't listening to me…"

"The most important point is that we understand *why* Caden is upset. At times, his perspective is skewed.

I have learned to start by acknowledging his perspective first by listening and inviting him to share more, all without my comment or judgment.

Once the door is open to his emotions, then we discuss his feelings.

When he can discuss how he feels, then we dig deeper into the story to determine if we need to take action."

Avoid a meltdown before it occurs

Establishing rituals can be an effective way to avoid an overwhelming meltdown before it occurs. Perhaps your child would enjoy a daily walk with one or both parents; playing with a pet; riding a bike; special reading time; or another calming activity. Any of these activities allow an emotional child to find their center and reground to their home environment.

If your child seems irritated about a specific situation, establish a set amount of time for your child to vent his frustration, take 10 minutes to close his eyes and do deeper breathing or yogic stretching exercises, or moving gently to music, which soothes nervous emotions. Set a timer for these activities. Once that time is up, agree that it is time to move on to the next task of homework, chores, having dinner, or walking the dog. Here is how Lucy handles such situations in her household.

Once in a while, 10-year-old Jordan comes home from school after witnessing one kid bully another or someone picking on another. Such an incident makes him sad and can turn into depression if he dwells on the insensitivity of his classmates.

Lucy acknowledges her son's feelings, but knows he has to do his homework and then attend his scout meeting with his dad. Lucy says to Jordan, "I understand you had a rough day and are frustrated. Because you have homework and a meeting tonight, why don't I set the timer on the microwave for three minutes so you can vent your frustration about the bullies in your class?" Lucy follows through and gives Jordan three minutes to be angry, frustrated, and annoyed. Once the timer beeps, Lucy tells Jordan, "Okay your three minutes are up; it's time to do your homework." Through this activity, Jordan does a good job of shifting his moods and regaining his focus. Lucy has used time as a boundary for Jordan's empathy. If he dwelt too long in his moodiness, depression would set in for days.

Setting boundaries for an emotionally empathic child

Setting energetic boundaries are important as well. Because empathic children are so sensitive and their emotions seem to bubble at the surface, it can be difficult for parents to set boundaries and stick with them.

For Tara's son Caden, his greatest challenge is accepting the different rules for himself and his older brother, Adam, who is four years older and has started middle school. Tara shares how she is constantly challenged by Caden's lack of understanding about the differences in the two boys' privileges.

"It is a constant struggle with Caden when it comes to the activities Adam is allowed to do and Caden is not. Every time Adam goes off to play with his friends and Caden is not invited to go, he gets upset. He always says it's not fair and I acknowledge why he feels that way.

On one occasion Adam left to play football and didn't invite Caden to go. Caden repeatedly asked me to let him go, and I reminded him that he was not invited. He continued to press me to call Adam, and I consistently replied, "Adam did not invite you to go; it's not my place to give you permission." When I told Caden he could not go, my words led to another mini meltdown.

The hardest thing for me as a parent was not to allow myself to give into his upset. I know Caden felt the loss of his brother, as it happened abruptly with the shift to middle school, and it was hard for me to see him cry his grief, but he needs to be equipped with management tools to navigate the real world. In addition, I have to respect my older son's right to be off playing with his friends."

Restoring personal strength

The International Resilience Project put forth A Guide to Promoting Resilience in Children: Strengthening the Human Spirit. *In this book, the author, Goldberg, suggests that children can draw from three sources of resilience. The first is to know what is available to them. The second resource is their inner personal skills, and the third resource is the action they can take. The three resources are reflected in statements for each category:*

I HAVE represents what is available in their environment.

I AM statements reflect the child's resources.

I CAN statements represent what the child could do, what action feels right.

I HAVE

A big brother who supports me and loves me.

My dog, Max, who sleeps on my bed when I feel upset.

My family who love me.

I AM

A sensitive person who likes to help others.

Happy most of the time.

Willing to be responsible for what I do.

I CAN

Share my feeling with my parents when I am overwhelmed.

Shift my moods from sad to happy.

Take 10 deep breaths to calm down and focus.

"A resilient child does not need all these features to be resilient, but one (set of skills) is not enough. Resilience results from a combination of these features."[2]

The need for champions

Children from emotionally toxic environments who are conditioned to fail can feel it to be a life sentence. We may see this trait in tweens and teens that have internalized the ill effects of negative emotions, injustice, or violence and developed issues such as anxiety, depression, aggressive responses to people or animals, hyperactivity, and over-reactivity. Perhaps the most devastating response to see is no response at all. The empathic intuitive child's withdrawal creates a condition like a volcano slowly building up the force to expel anger or hurt tucked away throughout the years.

We cannot overemphasize how important character development is in the home environment that a child develops by modeling and communicating with a mentor. As a parent, friend, or child's caregiver, you might become the champion, the mentor to an intuitive child. Eliza's story shows how critically important this role is for an intuitive to gain confidence and develop resilience by having someone appreciate her gifts and listen to her stories.

Eliza's story

Eliza Rey (*www.elizarey.com*), an intuitive, counsels others through her intuitive gifts. She was an intuitive child and is now the mother of two intuitive children. Eliza works as an occupational therapist with sensitive children in the schools and has a private counseling practice. Her vision is that all children have the freedom to develop their intuitive gifts with social acceptance so they do not feel strange, wrong, isolated, or fearful.

This is Eliza's story:

When I was 4, I was in bed and felt someone standing outside my window, which was right next to the bed. I tried to scream, but nothing came out of my mouth. My mom, dad, and brothers couldn't hear me. I was petrified night after night after night. Finally this feisty redhead had had enough. I was going to look out the window and see what was there. I can still see the face, like a witch with black hair.

I was out of bed in a flash and ran to my parents' room. My dad slept like a rock. My mother treated me like I was making it up, that it was my imagination. She was pulling my hair, saying nothing was in the house. The whole scene and her reaction terrified me more.

I got away from her and slept in my younger brother's twin bed. I learned my first intuitive tool, which is when you're afraid, go to a place of comfort or be with someone with whom you're comfortable. Cuddle up so you can feel the warmth of their body and put the warm blankets on you so you can have that relaxation.

When I was 8 years old, I spent the night with a friend who lived in an old home from the 1920s. I couldn't go in this one bathroom or several other rooms because when I did, I couldn't breathe. I finally said, "I have to go to the bathroom!" at 2 a.m. and ran to the nearest one. I saw an old woman in the bathtub under water. I ran out fast, again terrified.

I told my friend that I had a dream. By age 8, I had learned to substitute the word *dream* for *vision* because it was more acceptable. My friend told her mom what Lizzie saw, and her mom replied, "Oh, that's interesting, because the lady that lived here before, she drowned in that bathtub." So, one of my first clues that there was a reality to my visions was good, but I still couldn't talk about it!

Finally at 16-years-old I had empowerment. I felt like someone was next to me in my bed as I woke up at 2 or 3 a.m.. The moment I opened my eyes, I thought what I saw was a real life person who somehow got into the house. Then I realized this was a spirit form, and it said to me, "Don't worry, I won't hurt you." I developed again that extreme fear, and I left my body and was staring at myself in bed from the ceiling.

Okay, if this was what it's like to die, this was pretty cool. No pain, you're light, you're free, everything's fast. Then I fell back into my body. You know what? Being on the other side was a wonderful feeling. Why was I afraid all these years? Also in those years, I learned to predict when people would die. I learned that what I was feeling and hearing was not my imagination, and that this could help people, warn people. My grandmother was getting ready to pass. Grandpa came to me in a dream and was reaching out to Grandma, and I asked what he was doing. He said to tell Grandma that he was coming for her. I did, because I was close to my Grandma. She thanked me for letting her know and said she was glad to be with her husband soon.

Grandma was my comfort in my lifetime. She listened with a patience that I admire even now as an adult. Her appreciation of my little experiences led me to know I could help people.

This became even more important after my brother and father passed away when I was 18 years old. They had a tragic accident and were missing for a year. I knew they were dead, but I still felt their energy strongly around me.

Through my creative outlets, acceptance of my intuitive gifts, and the love and support of a few family members, I came to terms with why I was intuitive and how I am able to share my gifts for the betterment of others.

"How can my experiences help children today?" is a question I hear often. Here are some of my suggestions:

- We want to be in agreement with ourselves as parents that these children have abilities.
- Next, help them accept it in themselves. Form or sponsor play groups for intuitive children.
- These kids need to connect with an intuitive mentor, someone older who knows and can coach and validate them.
- Allow them the opportunity to draw, paint, and be musical. So many of these kids have wonderful creative urges.
- Listen to their stories. Don't tell them that what they are going through is their imagination. When you start telling a child that it is their imagination, you've lost their trust. They are going to find someone else to talk to.

The heart connection

In few cultures have emotions been given the permission to feel or freely express. We are afraid of being hurt by anger, sucked in by vulnerability, or dumped on by rage. Mostly we use words to express emotions rather than gestures, music, dance, art, or touch.

In the meantime, the empathic intuitive reads people's emotions clearly, senses the underlying feelings, and scans body language and facial features for congruence. What the empath tunes into may be comfortable or not, which underlies the need for emotional management skills for intuitive children.

We've learned in previous chapters that neuroscience has mapped how the whole brain processes information in four ways: feeling, sensing, intuition, and thinking. New research from the psychology of heart transplants showed us how intelligent hearts are emotional centers and make intelligent decisions for our comfort. Intuitive children can use this understanding to their benefit.

The heart and brain connection starts in-utero. From fetal heart cells grows a neural tube. The brain develops on the other end. Our heart grows connections with the brain and central nervous system and they communicate with each other constantly. An intuitive child or parent can use the heart energy to gauge clarity of their feelings and how to interpret them.

HeartWise

"Heart Math's findings point to the human heart as playing a key role in the intuitive process, and a recent study concludes the heart actually receives intuitive information faster than the brain—by a second or slightly more."[3]

A calming exercise is a physical activity like breathing or a mental exercise like visualization that helps one relax. Calming is a basic survival skill, an absolute must-have tool, for an intuitive child, especially the empath. An intuitive listens to intuition best when calm, not rushed. A creative child learns best when he can focus calmly. The following three strategies provide a calming influence and help an intuitive parent or child to focus better. A calm heart has a soothing influence on the brain and the whole central nervous system. Intuitive children can calm anxiety, excitation, or distraction easily.

- *Place their right palms on their chests and breathe slowly for several minutes. When they feel the neck and shoulders relax, they've arrived!*

- *Touching the heart, imagine an elevator in their heads. They enter the elevator when the doors open, push the heart-shaped button, and feel the movement down through the throat into the chest. The doors open, they step out into their heart, and remain there in silence for a while.*

- *As a parent, teach your child to find answers in his heart and his head. Show him that logic and intuition are not opposites. As a teacher, Caron gathered large, flat river stones, and the students in her class either wrote or drew a head on one side and heart on the other. When they had to make a personal choice about studies or peer or family matters, they turned the stone face up on either side, and asked their head or heart as designated. They got to explore two answers: the logical and the intuitive, and then discussed options. This proactive way to help solve a problem is easily used by teachers or parents.*

Chapter Review

- Empathic feelers have acute mental or emotional sensibilities, and as children, want to be responsive to other people's feelings. Yet, at times, their sensitivity threshold is low.
- Our children need confidence and the ability to focus and negotiate in the real world.
- An empath's vulnerability can also be their challenge in an emotionally toxic home where they may learn to cut off feelings.
- All children need a champion, and empathic children need an especially caring champion.
- Through empathic touch, you teach an intuitive child to trust his sense of feeling and body's messages.
- Touch is one key to regulate and support an intuitive child's physiology and communicate calm and strength to the nervous system.
- As a parent, friend, or child's caregiver, you are the first teacher of self-confidence and resilience.
- Calming is a basic survival skill, an absolute must-have tool, for an intuitive child. An intuitive listens to intuition best when calm, not rushed.

12

The Power of Optimistic Emotion

Managing our emotions increases intuition and clarity. It helps us self-regulate our brain chemicals and internal hormones. It gives us natural highs, the real fountain of youth we've been searching for. It enables us to drink from elixirs locked within our cells, just waiting for us to discover them.

—Doc Childre

Intuitives cultivate optimism

The power of optimism in intuitive children's lives is paramount because this attitude is the facilitator of positive emotional interactions. Optimistic children have better ability to bounce back from sadness and are more resistant to depression. Optimism has layers of meaning and the definition depends on your family's personal values. These may include:

- Hopefulness.
- Knowing clouds have silver linings.
- Good will prevail.
- Belief in a successful outcome.
- Confidence and cheerfulness.

Intuitive children's needs extend beyond what most parents today dealt with in their own upbringing. Children have sensitivity to environmental influences, foods, toys, clothing, noise levels, and the feelings of people around them. Because of such daily challenges, optimism is the key attitude to help intuitives stay confident and be sure of themselves, whether they feel deeply, or are artistic or creative thinkers.

Because intuitive children tend to be right-brain thinkers or holistic-type thinkers, they are mistakenly diagnosed as having attention deficit problems or hyperactive disorders or mood disorders. The authors stand strongly united in asking you to not drug your children with prescription medications until after you have read this book and have an opportunity to practice natural strategies for managing energies.

Identifying needs and moods

Our task is to coach our children in how to identify their needs and moods and find answers and solve problems by using their intuition. These are their primary needs:

- Connection or bond with someone they can trust deeply.
- An accepting heart to listen and acknowledge their psychic stories, creative impulses, or emotional depths.
- Avoidance of having their emotions pushed down.
- Acknowledgment of what they have to share as unique.
- Having an advocate for intuitives/avoiding labels and diagnoses.
- Possible alternative diet and schooling options.
- Boundaries to offset their tendency to absorb others' feelings.
- Models for values such as honesty, communication, and respect.

There is no way around optimism being a firm foundational attitude for intuitive children because it provides perspective. When Margaret saw the storm clouds around her father's head and associated that with anger, a different perspective could have been to understand the relationship between alcoholism and anger. She may even have mentioned it to him when he wasn't drinking beer.

A different perspective for an empath who feels the sting of parents' arguing is to find an alternative way to transform that sting by changing activities, environments, or finding someone to discuss feelings with. Optimism encourages us to seek the challenge, solution, or negotiation.

> ### Take an optimism break
>
> *If you need a mood shift, a shot of vitality, or energy boost, try these sure, fire activities:*
>
> 1. *Give a hand. Give of your time. Doing something nice for another person focuses your attention on sharing heart. Giving feels generous and compassionate.*
>
> 2. *To restore your soul, immerse yourself in nature. How long has it been since you climbed a tree, built a sandcastle, took a wilderness retreat, or enjoyed a solitary hike with your child?*
>
> 3. *Fill your room with music that makes you smile and soar!*

When we first suggested mood management to an audience, one mom protested that she would never control her children. We agreed that a parents' role is not controller. To be clear, then, our task as parents with an empath is *help* children to:

- Identify their feelings or emotions.
- Be able to separate their emotions from another's.
- Manage emotional outbursts or energy that is harmful to the self or others.
- Maintain an optimistic attitude.

Many strategies are based on two techniques, (1) modeling and (2) showing, which are natural to children. The approaches empower children to reach goals of being confident and learning to successfully negotiate their environment. To manage means to

- be in charge.
- maintain control.
- have influence over.
- oversee or handle.

What greater gift can we model than to be in charge of one's life? Tara presents her management solutions for each of her two sons who express their emotions differently. Notice how each of the children's intuitive insights differ according to how each perceives and interacts with their individual environments.

Managing moods

Tara shares: "Adam is 11 years old. As a coach for parents, I recognize that Adam's style for handling emotions requires that he have a physical release for the energy as it surges through his body. His predisposition is to act things out through his behavior. Depending on what he is feeling, he will display impatience, as in becoming easily frustrated or quick to temper, if something is bothering him, or, will become hyperactive, bouncing off the walls, if he has been affected by foods or too much time playing video games or watching television. Some may view hyperactivity as an early sign of ADHD, but my key has been to find creative ways to help him manage his energy surges for the benefit of his long-term well being.

"**Effective Strategies for Impatience and Energy Surges:** Adam has learned to use his physical skills to burn off steam in sports activities, Tae Kwon Do, and a yoga-stretching program. We taught him to breathe deeply for his high activity, which calmed his nervous system so he could manage his energy on his own.

"Bringing a child's attention to their bodily feelings helps children identify them. They can sharpen intuitive skills by becoming aware of the places in their body that are triggered by environmental stimuli around them."

Acknowledgment, pause, shift

When you are feeling upset, acknowledge the emotion and shift the feeling before you interact with your intuitive child. We all feel anger and frustration at times. Many of us react in the moment based on how we feel, which can lead to a disconnection with our child. My mom gave me advice years ago to always stop and count to 10 before I responded to one of my kids. It sounded great in theory. Often emotion comes on so strongly and the thought of counting to 10 doesn't even enter my mind. My mom probably repeated those words often before it sunk in. The point is to respond, rather than react. It takes practice to be aware and ask yourself the following questions:

- *What feelings are running in your body?*
- *What thoughts are in your head?*
- *Are they the feelings and words you want to express to your child?*

> *It does take practice, and the first few times you respond with the old pattern, make it okay! Parenting is an evolutionary process and the first step to transforming anything is to acknowledge it.*

Tara discusses her mood management of her second intuitive son, Caden.

At age 7, Caden is an intuitive, empathic child. He is hypersensitive to the emotions of the people around him, especially the children in his classroom. One day after school, he came home in a low mood. During the afternoon, he experienced three emotional outbursts about seemingly small things. After my attempts to find out what was triggering him, he said that he was upset about a little boy in his class who was in trouble with the teacher.

How did we come to this specific conclusion? The issues that occurred during his afternoon would appear small to most of us. Someone threw his tennis ball out in the yard for a dog to fetch; he was tackled while playing football; another child made a remark that would normally not bother him. To others, these scenarios would be normal for kids playing.

How it is different for Caden is that he tells the story from his perspective, how it happened to him. This connected the dots for my understanding how he empathically identifies with others. I notice that when he is describing something he witnessed, he tells how it felt for him. Once he finishes his story I asked, "This didn't happen to you, did it?" He told me the event happened to a friend named Ricky.

This is a classic example of a child who is empathic. Caden feels a situation he is witnessing like it is happening to his own body. So what techniques did we use and what was the outcome?

Effective Strategies for an empathetic child: "My best approach with Caden is logical. So I start by asking questions, 'What is causing you to feel this way?' or, 'Why are you so angry?' My questions call attention to his moods. He doesn't usually know what caused his emotional upset, which is why we need to talk about it, so he will:

- Tell a story of how it felt or happened directly to him.
- Tell a story from another's vantage point.

Calming techniques also work when Caden can't verbalize what was causing the emotional outbursts.

Once we identify what caused the energy to bottle up, we apply some or more of the following methods to move the emotion out of his system.

Warm, relaxing baths work well for Caden. He will spend an hour or more in water, a balm for his fired-up nervous system.

Other techniques he uses to manage energy on his own are quiet time away from his siblings like building with blocks. In warmer weather he grounds himself by going barefoot in the yard and playing in the dirt."

Positive emotional atmosphere

Parents model for children how to respond emotionally to others. For the empathic child, emotional boundaries are an issue. So our goal for a child with empathy is to help them find internal strength to be positive and proactive, not reactive or regretful. Our children can thrive in their intuitive resourcefulness and feel competent to use intuition to make peace, develop a plan, or solve a problem.

The fact is that all parents strive to learn from their children and see through their eyes. A truer statement is that parents of an empathic or sensitive child *have to know* how their child experiences emotional energy. The situations scream for intuitive, aware, and compassionate parents to become responsible to their kids and teach them emotional management skills.

Healthy home ambiance

Atmospheres are crucial determinants of the life force. A positive and caring atmosphere fosters open minds, healthy emotions, and clear intuitive skills. A healthy home atmosphere is founded on how we interact with each other. The following suggestions are verbs, words of doing, and actions for all family members.

- *Showing respect through communication and kindness looks like asking, not demanding, actions or answers.*

- *Caring is shown through listening, expressing affection, showing love, and doing service for another.*
- *Respecting limits and boundaries usually neutralizes tension and conflict, the cause of bullying in families.*
- *Developing each person's talents through practice, praise, and persistence raises self-confidence.*
- *Working or playing together by creating projects, rituals, camping trips, or pet care schedules support a cooperative team effort.*
- *Creating healthy habits together by defining menus, planning meals, or assigning chores provides support for modeling good choices.*

Basic management skills for intuitives

Self-restraint: In the first few seconds that we see something, our impressions may not be accurate, as the brain tries to find the associated memory. So when our children see a ghost or feel another's emotions, we can help them clarify their interpretations of the incident. Acting solely on emotional information can cause a faulty response like jumping to conclusions, taking opinions as fact, or having the wrong answers. Always check emotional responses with the physical facts and with the intuition. Our bodies are designed for checks and balances. This excellent management skill helps children think through their responses before jumping to conclusions.

Indispensable emotional feelings: Empathic children may be more emotional about their decisions; yet emotions are crucial to decision-making. Always check with your intuitive child before making big decisions that affect them. Check with their emotions and check-in with their intuition on the matter. An opportunity opened in a new magnet school for the arts for 13-year-old Shelley. The school principal called Shelley's mom to say that her name had been picked from the lottery of students in classrooms for the gifted. Shelley's mom thought the opportunity for her artistic daughter rocked and immediately said, "Yes." Later the mom checked her intuition to make sure this was the right decision for her daughter's highest good. Great, her intuition said that it was. Then Shelley returned home from camp. When she heard what her mother had agreed to, she stomped her feet and ran to her room with a resounding, "No." Shelley valued her friends and her comfort level in her peer group at her previous school. In her mind she could take art any time.

Shelley's mom made her attend the magnet school and Shelley lasted there about two weeks before coming home in tears of misery because she missed her friends. Their values clashed. Mom jumped to a decision based on wanting her daughter's creativity to be nurtured. At 13, nothing was more important to Shelley than her other intuitive friends with whom she could be real, empathic, and weird. Shelley's needs as an intuitive were more important than her mom's plans for her.

- **Focusing:** A way to improve intuition is by focusing, which is based on our inherent, natural ability to become aware of our bodily senses. The following focus exercises provide direct access to a body knowing by entering the feeling. The result of focusing is immediate transformation or shifting. The following suggestions below are for dealing with emotions. We will also discuss focusing in the chapter on children with psychic gifts.

- Perhaps your intuitive child broods or suddenly has an explosive outbreak. Start the focus process by calming down or centering together. Emotions are not logical, so before asking questions, take a calming moment to connect feelings with reasoning.

- Start by asking questions about what bothers him. Don't give up; allow your child the time needed to verbally communicate what might be bothering him.

- If he can't identify a cause, ask, "Where in your body do you feel it? Place your hand there."

- Wait in silence. Don't push. Give your child's intuition time to work.

- Intuition holds answers. A child simply has to access it, so assume your child does know the answer and help him find it.

- Intuition always has an answer, so if the tension builds a little, that is good. If the reply is, "I don't know," then move through these options to take the pressure off, but maintain the tension:

- ➤ "Take a guess. Put your hand where you guess it is."
- ➤ "Thanks mind. It's okay you don't know. The hand knows, and the hand can find it. Go ahead hand."
- ➤ "Okay, just make up where you feel it in your body and put your hand there."

- We celebrate the naming of the feeling because now the feeling is familiar. The child knows it. What we know, we can deal with.

- Focus offers your child the opportunity to shift moods and make choices about how to deal with it. Ask the feeling what action to take or ask your child to make a logical decision about how to get the results he wants.

- **Change the environment.** Redirecting attention is the opposite of focusing. To break an emotional circuit of tension, anger, or upset, move to a different activity or environment. Suggest a bath, a swim in the pool, quiet time playing with a favorite toy, exercise or take a walk, read together, or watching a sunset. Shifting your child out of the emotion of the moment is important so she does not continue to feed *her own* energy into a negative situation.

- **Teach your children to breathe deeper.** Shallow breathing creates tension. When your child can calm his nervous system down enough to breathe, the emotion physically dissolves from his body. (Refer to chapter on shifting moods for further breathing instruction.)

- **Practice heart-centering.** Sit with your child quietly and ask your child to bring his awareness to his heart. By doing this both of you shift your child's energy to a warm, peaceful space. Once you each feel centered, then discuss the problem, check intuition, connect, and bond.

Chapter Review

- Because of daily challenges, optimism is the key to help intuitives stay confident and be sure of themselves, whether they feel deeply, or are artistic or creative thinkers.

- Our task is to coach our children in how to identify their needs and moods, and shift to more positive or optimistic states if necessary.

- Optimism enables an intuitive to be optimal, and we can cultivate the attitude of seeing the whole picture and connecting with people who promote positive energy.

- Bringing a child's attention to their bodily feelings helps them identify their energetic influxes. They can sharpen intuitive skills by becoming aware of the places in their body that are triggered by environmental stimuli around them.

- Parents model for children how to respond emotionally to others. For the empathic child, emotional boundaries are an issue. So our goal for a child with empathy is to help them find internal strength to be positive and proactive, not reactive or regretful.

- Atmospheres are crucial determinants of the life force. A positive and caring atmosphere fosters open minds, healthy emotions, and clear intuitive skills. A healthy home atmosphere is founded on how we interact with others.

- Basic management skills include self-restraint, focusing, acknowledgement of emotions and their role, shifting physical environments, relieving tension through deeper breathing, and heart-centering.

13

Spiritual Foundation and Connection

True wisdom comes to each of us when we realize how little we understand about life, ourselves, and the world around us.

—Socrates

Nurturing spiritual intelligence

Is our spiritual nature inherent or do we learn it? How do we develop a sense of wonder or a connection to that which is greater than ourselves that we call god, great mystery, spirit, or source? Spiritual intelligence has three characteristics:

1. A sense of finding or knowing the meaning or direction in our lives.
2. A connection to something greater than ourselves.
3. A sense of inner peace or internal centering derived from a bond beyond our five senses.

Children with strong spiritual intelligence understand that they have a purpose in life. Their learning and interests revolve around discovering this purposeful pursuit. They also describe an inner connection that brings them peace or confidence. Nurturing their intuitive intelligence strengthens their connection and broadens their empathy and creativity. In this chapter, we'll explore the link between intuitive intelligence and spiritual intelligence and discuss how intuition correlates with spirituality.

145

Natural Intelligences	Plus Intuitive Intelligence =
Physical Prowess Enhanced by Intuitive Intelligence	
Physical	*Learns by doing, has exceptional kinesthesia, motor skills, sense of timing, and movement with the body.*
Creative, Inspired Intuitive	
Mental-Creative	*Inspired, inventive, creative, follows inner music, ideas, and actions motivated by internal genius. Can daydream, be distracted, learns to focus, and learns through experimentation.*
Empathic Intuitive	
Emotional-Social	*Reads others, feels others, defines self in relation to others. Needs boundaries, emotional management skills, self-identification, and confidence.*
Psychic Intuitive	
Intuitive	*Expanded awareness of the nonphysical worlds or subtle energy fields through receptors in the biochemistry. Exhibits talents of subtle knowing, hearing, seeing, telepathy, and other talents.*
Spiritual Intuitive	
Spiritual	*Intuition serves kids with spiritual intelligence as the doorway and interpreter to connection with inner worlds.*

Spirituality is a subset of spiritual intelligence

We define spirituality in this book as a belief in a power greater than ourselves. Spirituality can be part of a designated religion, a self-directed exploration of consciousness or feeling connected to nature. Spirituality or being spiritual is a subset of the spiritual intelligence domain. Spirituality is a skill set we can teach and learn. Spiritual behaviors that all children might beneficially learn include how to pray and meditate, consider ethics or morals, and build empathy through service.

On the other hand, a child's natural spiritual intelligence includes an awareness of inner worlds, self-directed and independent seeking of the connection, and a feeling of peace or awe. On the chart of natural intelligences, we are exploring the intuitive child who has exceptional spiritual intelligence manifesting as purpose, passion, and connection and caring.

Imagine climbing a mountain and arriving at the 10,000-foot peak. You stop, inhale the fresh air and stand in awe of the surrounding scenery. In a sense, in that spiritual moment, you are being the mountain experience.

Children with an inner drive for that mountain experience will make the climb and find it exhilarating. They are willing to put effort into the climb, having faith that the end experience justifies their effort and energy. During the climb, they may show fatigue or fear of failure, yet they persevere. An inner drive motivates them to pursue their goal. Bouncing back after a setback, these children are remarkably resilient in their attitudes and motivations.

There is just one great spiritual teacher, and that is the Divine Spirit in your heart. What any spiritual teacher on the outside can do, at best, is to always lead you back to that teacher in your heart.

From a Dialogue with Brother David Steindl-Rast, *"A Revolution of Authority" in* What Is Enlightenment, *Issue 9.*

To summarize, spiritual intelligence is a natural temperament, which appears as the primary interactive style in a developing child. Author and transpersonal therapist, Frances Vaughn, described traits of spiritual intelligence as

- concerned with inner life and its relationship to being in the world.
- deeper insight into levels of consciousness.
- awareness of our relationship to the transcendent, each other, Earth, and all beings.[1]

Melissa's story

Melissa F. Halsey, clairvoyant and spiritual counselor of wisdom teachings (*wisdomword.com*) started a waking-up process two years before she became pregnant. She felt a strong desire to protect children. During this time, she worked as an elementary arts teacher for the gifted and talented in Long Island, New York.

In Melissa's words:

About a year before and during my pregnancy the plight of the world's children caused me grief. Everywhere I looked and in my dreams, I saw gaunt, sad-eyed children reaching out for help. I questioned the condition of the world that we were creating for children to live and grow in. I wondered how I was to raise this child in my belly and why I was bringing her into this world where there were already so many in need.

When my daughter was born in 1983, I felt strangely different inside. I kept trying to convey this to my friends and family. I felt like I was in a glass bowl with everyone else on the other side, unable to clearly see or hear me.

Clarity and peace finally filtered in when night after night I found myself comfortably cocooned with my daughter in an old fashioned rocking chair, nursing her. I'd look into her eyes and ask, "Who are you?" and "What did you come here to teach me?" The question and the gaze from those steady deep, blue eyes brought a sense of peace, and then, amusement at myself, as these questions weren't ones that I would ask ordinarily.

I was conservative, very Westchester, go-to-college, get a good job, make a better life for yourself and your children type person. These feelings and language were unusual for me.

At the time I attributed the origin of the questions to two things. First, sitting still and quiet for extended periods of time in the silence of the night without a task, something to do or perform, or somebody to take care of—this was a totally novel experience for me. Second I attributed my new awareness to the natural opening of one who is doing something meditative. For me nursing my daughter was meditative.

Six months of quiet brought me deeper into my self, raising questions about life, spirit, and the universe. I also met other people who were recognizing the same issues and had feelings similar to mine.

When my daughter was a toddler, I thought about leaving my marriage. I had concern that I was leaving it for selfish pursuit of a spiritual path that I felt compelled to follow. My husband and I were discussing this over breakfast in the kitchen nook while the toddler played on the floor around us. Suddenly she crawled over to me, climbed up on the chair, and put her cheek next to mine. She looked at her dad and said, "I go where my mama goes, and I do my mama's work." Our jaws dropped open and we were speechless for a long moment.

That is how this little one would communicate with us through the years. One minute, she was a wise being; the next, she was back to being a kid. We'd shake our heads asking, "Did she just say that?" She did this several times as a child and she continues to do that into her 20s.

In the first few months after her birth, recognition in my daughter's eyes stirred me to think and feel in new ways. In the toddler years, her knowing showed in her statements of truth when she made eye contact and spoke confidently in an adult way. Once, after I had left the marriage and moved out of state, her dad was visiting and commenting about how far away we lived. She brought her ball over to her dad, held it up, and said, "If ever anyone is on the ball, they're always together if they're together in the heart." The sudden shifts from happy-go-lucky child to wise being led me to believe that these powerful adult statements were strictly intuitive.

Another aspect of intuitive clarity was her desire, maybe even demand, for horses. This started when she was a preverbal toddler and has influenced her entire life. She didn't want dolls or toys. She wanted horses—miniaturized plastic replica statues, such as the Breyer Horse collection, which older children usually wanted.

Once, a woman, a horse trainer, was visiting the house. My daughter was playing quietly on the floor and pointing to different parts of the horse's anatomy, clearly naming them: withers, hocks, and flanks. The woman said to me, "Boy, you taught your daughter well about the parts of a horse." I told her I didn't teach her these words because I knew nothing about them." We had a shocked moment as we wondered how a 2-year-old would know these terms when she was not exposed to them at all. As she grew older, horses and all animals continued to be her passion.

Her school years and interaction with peers caused her to experience an impatience and frustration. Then there were emotional issues. Because I had started channeling after she was born, one solution was for her to talk to the angels and guides that I channeled. This was easier for her than speaking to me and allowed her to understand feelings and perceptions. It was also easier for me, as I took her frustrations less personally. If she spoke to me, her anger or my need to have everything perfect might have overwhelmed both of us.

This helped us deal with the ups and downs of her school years where conventional methods couldn't. What she felt and came to accept was that she was different; that it was all right to be so, and that the school system didn't teach the way she learned. At this stage of the game, this special woman is 25 years old, happy, beautiful, and self-sufficient. She knows how to handle people and handle herself. Because people can sometimes be clouded with untruths and confusion, she finds animals and horses rarely are.

Reflections on empathy

Melissa continues: "My daughter was an intuitive child who read people and felt what they felt. She was irritated to find that people didn't express their bottled up feelings and thoughts. This confused her. So, if she was speaking with an angry adult who pretended happiness, she felt the anger and could "run it," even becoming enraged. Imagine how she felt in a classroom of angry teens or in a school with frustrated teachers? I think her direct personality doesn't allow for dissembling in people. Her kinesthetic nature valued authenticity and still does. She's not easily deceived. For a child like this the traditional educational methods never worked."

Reflections for parents of intuitive children

By Melissa Halsey

"The skills that you need to deal with these special beings or what you learn from dealing with them is to be sure of yourself. Be clear about who you are as a parent and what energy you're putting into the world. Having an intuitive child forced my authenticity at an early stage in motherhood. I couldn't deny my spiritual gifts or my daughter's intuition.

"The different intuitive children and parents I've worked with are forced to acknowledge and deal with their sensitive talents. These spiritual children in the adult's lives seem to crack open their sensitivities. Then this brings up the other side of the coin, which is the painfulness of being sensitive or an empath in a harsh and chaotic world that makes no place for them. My answer for dealing with this was developing a deep spiritual connection, and those individuals I counsel also seek that deeper connection, that intuition. To me, this is a marriage between spiritual intelligence and intuitive intelligence.

"For example, there is the pain of being weird and feeling different for an intuitive adolescent. There is also the pain of being teased and taunted by peers. The peer pressure to fit in and be accepted causes kids to smash down their individuality and go for the crowd mentality. The peer group suppresses individuality; intuition and creativity are lost or redirected for survival.

> *"Unless a parent can understand the depth of the child's feeling, they might not recognize the child's gifts. If they can't understand their offspring's turmoil, they might be tempted to say, 'Why can't you be like everybody else or why can't you just suck it up and move forward." These children know better than to suck it up. Sometimes their integrity won't let them do that. I know one parent who totally provides money for any spiritual mentoring or support for her child, but she doesn't know her child's truth and talents. They found a way to have a relationship. The parent loves the child and makes sure she has therapy or mentors. Any special child who finds a mentor that can provide a stable reflection for individuality and creativity can find their way. A spiritual intuitive needs validation and loving acceptance."*

Feeling connected

For spiritually intelligent children, feeling connected must start early in life with a sense of belonging and matures into the value of relationships or an inner sense of purpose.

For infants, the earliest connecting comes from touch and a loving bond with a primary caretaker. The experience includes bonding, movement, and soothing words of his or her parents, all of which are crucial for the developing infant to form neural pathways for positive connections. The infant learns to attend by focusing on the sounds of the parents and their gazes and smiles. In short, the child knows himself through sensory connection to the caregiver.

Valuing connection

Children first value their connections with primary caregivers and later their families. We show how we value a child in so many ways, from our smiles throughout the day to the appreciation we verbalize. This is **most important:** *How* we value and show respect for children provides their models for how they will recognize and value themselves. The quality of our relationships and interactions with our children impact their physiology and provide the foundation for developing spiritual virtues.

When bonding is successful in the early years, children develop healthy personalities and explore and play, take risks, and experience natural consequences. A self-directed child, who is competent in interactions and confident in decisions, emerges. A spiritual intuitive will feel free to explore his path, find his purpose, and seek the resources to fulfill it.

Trusting Adam

As a first-time parent with her oldest son Adam, Tara intuitively recognized her son's need to be trusted, respected, and validated for his inner strength and wisdom at a young age. Once she caught herself repeating some of the patterns of her own upbringing when her son Adam steadfastly protested that he was not lying. Tara explains: "In that moment I felt accused, just like Adam did now. When I was Adam's age, my mother accused me of lying to her when I hadn't. Then I was grounded for something I didn't do. Only in my adult years did I realize why I have had a lack of trust.

"I made a commitment to trust Adam when he told me he wasn't lying. As a child with a strong intuitive nature, Adam isn't prone to being dishonest with himself or others. I want to nurture his honesty.

"In that moment I restored trust, giving Adam the spiritual foundation to know he will be believed and that he can be honest no matter what happens."

Children with spiritual intelligence

All children ask early in life about the spiritual mystery. Where did my dog go when he died? Why is grandpa in heaven? Can I touch the stars? Children with spiritual intelligence, however, seem never to stop asking such questions. Their wonder and deeper understanding of the world continues to unfold as they mature.

These children seem to be the "old souls" we refer to when we hear their wisdom and ponder their goodness. The children with spiritual intelligence don't turn it on and off. Their compassion is ingrained. Their connection to animals, nature, and to the hearts of people is real and consistent. Like Nelson Mandela, they are filled with a purpose to their lives. Like author

Dan Millman, they see the inner stirring of spirit and have peak experiences. Like Melissa's daughter, these altruistic children have their solitary way of approaching life, often without social conventions.

Spiritually intelligent children feel the mystery of life cycles and instinctively trust the mystery that exists. Situations change, and how children accept change depends on their feeling of connection. Spiritual intelligence provides a language of sacredness common to all disciplines and religions. Spiritual intelligence provides the faith to deal with adversity and a foundation of optimism all children will need in life. Sometimes so much change happens that children may feel that "something" out there is taking care of them. They survived. By such experiences, spiritually intelligent children develop an inner authority or wisdom. Getting to that wisdom is where intuitive intelligence is supportive.

Caden's story

From the time Tara's son Caden was an infant, the word she used to describe him was love. He has an amazing energetic presence that calms anyone who enters a room. When Caden was three, his first interaction with the non-physical world was seeing colors in his room at night. This was Tara's first experience with one of her children's psychic abilities. Rather than explain it away or allow fear to creep in, she responded to Caden by assuring him it was probably the Angels coming to see him. Tara shared how each angel had a unique color that represented different feelings. This was the first of many clairvoyant experiences her son would have. The most profound involved the sudden passing of Tara's father, Caden's beloved "papa."

Tara explains: "I remember Caden knocking on my dad's casket at his funeral and looking puzzled when he didn't knock back. Shortly after his death, Caden saw my father's energy every other day.

"A few months later, Caden lost his favorite blanket of four years. In an effort to comfort himself for the loss of my dad and his blanket, Caden convinced himself my dad had his blanket and took solace in this for two years."

Tara created a spiritual foundation for Caden by comforting him with stories about angels when he first saw them. This was strengthened when

Caden saw his grandpa after his death, which gave him the peace of knowing there is safety in the other dimensions he experiences. Caden soothed himself and found comfort when he lost his blanket by connecting the loss with his grandpa in a positive way. In his mind, he was connected to both.

Tips for spiritually connecting with your child

By Tara

- *View your child as a whole being capable of understanding things you may not yet know.*

- *Be willing to see your reflection in your child and recognize things your child may teach you.*

- *Follow rather than lead, as you learn to support the energies of your child.*

- *Pay attention to your child's behavior when they are around certain people. Children feel the energy of other people and if you ask them what it feels like to be around someone, they may share with you that someone made them feel light or heavy.*

- *Give yourself time to nurture your own needs. It is only when you allow yourself time to be in touch with your own spirit that you become aware of what's going on inside of and around you. Only through time for "you" can you fully live and demonstrate to children the gifts you want them to have. They must witness you "practicing what you preach."*

- *When your child feels anger, identify the emotion and demonstrate for your child how to move through the feeling so there is no unnecessary (negative) energy stored in the body. It is important for children to learn that anger is a normal feeling, but they need to move through the emotion so it doesn't show up later in life. Effective ways of managing the energy is as important as letting it go.*

- *When your child is upset or feels pain, whether you think he should feel the way he does or not, acknowledge his true feelings and explore the feeling with him. What your child feels at any moment is very real, and by telling a child they shouldn't feel that way, causes them to go inside and question whether they are allowed to feel what they are experiencing. What a child feels is their reality and they need to be supported in the moment. Pushing it down will cause it to resurface later in other situations or interactions with people.*

- *If you want your child to behave, expect that he will. Make sure you are not expecting your child to behave to meet someone else's expectations. Rely on your intuitive connection with your child to expect the best.*

- *Consider the qualities you want your child to have later in life and be careful not to push these qualities down in the present. It can be very challenging to keep in mind at a time of frustration, that later in life we want our kids to be independent, headstrong, and persistent. We need to nurture these characteristics as our children grow even when they are using them on us!*

- *Help your child recognize and foster his intuitive and special gifts by teaching awareness now, so he doesn't need to painfully relearn them later in life. We, as adults, spend years attempting to relearn what we knew as children.*

Link between intuition and spiritual intelligence

Children with high intuitive intelligence like Caden can be perceptive and psychic. Psychic gifts like the ability to hear inner direction, see into the nonphysical worlds, or sense and feel another's emotions are gifts of intuitive intelligence, but are not necessarily spiritual. A child can see ghosts without a sense of unity; they may be fearful and not equipped to handle the situation. Visions of the nonphysical world leave children at a loss of direction. Prediction of perceived dire future events may frighten them, causing withdrawal.

A child with spiritual intelligence can be better equipped from their inner connection to deal with the ghost. Intuitive children attuned to the nonphysical worlds may be distracted by it. A spiritual child attuned to the nonphysical worlds with intuition can find purpose within it.

Author Julie Tallard Johnson tells teens in her book, *Teen Psychic: Exploring Your Intuitive, Spiritual Powers* (2003), that claiming their intuition is about tapping into their inner "nagi," the spirit, soul, essence, or energy within each of us. In this interpretation, intuition, "going in-to-it," is the doorway to the inner spirit.

Intuition is a path into the sacred inner space of spiritual intelligence.

Deepak Chopra describes intuition as an attribute of our mind, the ability to understand the subtler mechanics, while spiritual intelligence encompasses the attributes of the heart.

Intuition is the interpreter of the qualities of spiritual intelligence.

Spiritual intelligence and intuition are intimately linked for a child who has strengths in both areas, providing checks-and-balances for their insight. For example:

- A child's altruistic heart might be too trusting, and a gut-level warning helps the child think through their impulses before acting.
- Spiritual inner wisdom helps an intuitive empath discern the boundaries between their feelings and that of someone to whom they are connected.

Children who have had spiritual experiences often describe the opening of intuitive gifts that were dormant. Jade, age 13, was a passenger in the family car that her sister was driving to the mall. The girls were going to shop for school clothes, but they never arrived. A drunk driver going too fast rear-ended the girls' car, catapulting them forward as the car leapt and landed hard. Jade's experience was an instant revelation that she was going headfirst into the windshield. As she felt herself flying out of her body, she saw a light, from which a hand extended and cushioned her momentum forward and guided her into her body. Next the hand guided her body to sit upright in the passenger's seat. Jade walked away from the accident without a scratch. From that day onward, Jade could see angels around people.

Finding their inner resources

Not all intuitive children believe parents when we say, "You are a strong kid! You can handle it! Find your strength, don't let them bully you." Children with whom we have worked appreciated the praise, but few knew how to use their intuition to access inner strength. We parents need to show them. Here is one way five boys found their inner resourcefulness, all in an afternoon exercise. As a teacher of special needs children who slipped through the school system's cracks, Caron's classroom on a Friday afternoon allowed students a time to turn inward. These kids were barely making it through school although they had normal or better intelligence. They were in a special needs classroom for specific issues such as emotional problems, mental health concerns, and learning disorders. Caron looked for a way to motivate them by discovering their interests, dreams, and ability to solve their own problems.

The boys in seventh grade sat in a circle on comfortable lounging pillows in the classroom. The exercise was for them to find the answer to the question: How can I work better in school? Their eyes were closed, and Caron had finished a three-minute relaxation exercise. She asked them to make themselves tiny, go inside their bodies, and find their strengths or ways to learn better. Surf the small currents of their blood. Slide up or down their spine slowly and smoothly, feeling the connection, seeking disconnects. Conduct a brain scan, and check the nerve impulses for consistency.

Chris's curious mind was fascinated. He jumped in first. "I found it. I found my disconnect. It is right below my shoulder blades, right on my spine, right where I was hurt in a car accident when I was a kid."

"Can you explain more?" Caron asked.

"Sure, I slid slowly down my spine, and when I got to that part, I noticed one of the nerve endings had loose ends [frayed]. I tried twisting it together, but that didn't work. So I held it and tried to figure it out. I couldn't figure it. So like you said, I pretended I had x-ray vision and sizzled it together. I know it can unwind again, so I have to go back in if I want to learn, and smooth out the edges a couple times a week. By the way, closing my eyes was real relaxing too."

Chris made a responsible choice to do this daily, especially before his math class each day. The ritual, using his creative mind and intuitive intelligence, provided a proactive focus for his learning skills. Moreover, he no longer felt like a dumb special education student.

Jerry was by far the most sensitive boy in the classroom. Gangly and tall, he towered over his peers. He shyly asked, "I don't know if I'm supposed to share this. Everybody will laugh."

"'Oh come on," Nathan yelled. "Maybe we will. Maybe we won't."

"Okay then, I saw my angel. He was tall and white, and he told me not to worry about school, but to do my best. If I did that, I would be okay."

"Hey weirdo," said Nathan. "I saw your angel too, but I thought I was making it up. He smiled at me."

I chimed in, "Thanks, Nathan, Chris, and Jerry. You guys have done great so far. Who's next...?"

Caron helped students use their intuition to strengthen their inner spirit, to help them get through their school year by feeling like they could participate. If spiritual children lose their connection to their spirit or optimism, the results are anxiety, depression, and an attitude of giving up.

Another example is 14-year-old Caitlin who had Hodgkin's disease. Caitlin also had a deep reservoir of spiritual strength and confessed that she felt helpless to fight her disease or know what to do. Caitlin's answers could only come from inside her heart. Caron asked her to place her hand on her heart to imagine that her heart had a voice. What did it sound like? What color did the voice speak with? What advice did the heart have for Caitlin about helping her body heal?

Caitlin's heart came up with several methods: writing funny stories about life in the hospital, starting a support group online where she could talk with other children in hospitals, and having a volunteer come to the hospital and read to her. Caitlin's parents helped her develop these suggestions into full-blown projects, which took Caitlin's attention and energy. As her passion grew, so did Caitlin's health. She beat Hodgkin's by participating proactively. Thanks to her intuitive suggestions, she created her life purpose, her spiritual purpose.

Critical need for spiritual foundations

Psychic children need a spiritual compass for their lives. The spiritual compass can be with a specific religion, spiritual philosophies or practices, thriving in nature, or even a loving connection in their social spheres. Their needs to belong and to pursue their missions are equally strong. How can we keep our knowing children in our hearts and set them free at the same time? The answer is in their spiritual foundation, returning to their inner wisdom voice, their heart's view for their life journey.

Wisdom Voice: To empower inner strength, we have always taught our children to find, listen, and trust their inner voices of wisdom. Give the voice of conscience any name: Wise Word, Star, Jake, Emma, God, Spirit, Friend, Angel, or Goodness. A name helps anchor the concept as a familiar in our children's brains. We also ask that children place their hand on the location in their body where they feel their inner wisdom. The emotional association between touch and wisdom helps them focus. Usually it is straightforward to ask questions and establish the foundation for the inner voice:

"Close your eyes or just relax and be quiet for a moment. Where in your body do you sense your special voice of wisdom? Place your hand there? Next describe the feeling to me." A voice of wisdom has a sense of humor, honesty, kindness, graciousness, and a positive approach to life. A voice of any other kind is not the wisdom voice. In this case, we keep searching. "You know, that voice sounds a little harsh (rude, bullying…) to me. Why don't we try again tomorrow and we'll fins a new place of wisdom in your body and see how that feels."

Heart's Voice: If children have difficulty finding a wisdom voice, then ask them to place their hand on their heart. Waiting several minutes for them to relax and get a feel for their heart, and then ask, "Heart, will you be John's wisdom voice?" Your child's heart usually responds with a yes.

We have noted two exceptions to this general rule: The first exception includes children who have been hurt or abused and feel too much pain in their heart. Thus, their heart might say no because they do not want to open the door to deeper feelings. A second exception is the intuitive empath who cries when she goes to her heart. Such children are reservoirs of emotion and could cry for joy or pain. In either case, we do not penetrate their heart feelings, which are private to them.

Empowering the Wisdom Voice: For an intuitive empath, an intuitive creative, a spiritual intuitive, or psychic, the voice of inner wisdom is their beacon to guide their choices. Get the heart's wisdom in how to handle a bully, what to say to a ghost, whether to swim with the dolphins, or how to report a peer for drug use. When children need your guidance, give it, but also ask them to check their inner wisdom. As a parent when your suggestion agrees with your child's choices, you won't clash in values and expectations. When parents and children, especially teens, both check in with their heart, you have room for discussion without emotional baggage. Moreover, your children will learn to trust their inner wisdom when you are not there for them.

Chapter Review

- Spiritual intelligence is a natural temperament, which appears as the primary interactive style in a developing child.
- Children with strong spiritual intelligence understand that they have a purpose in life. Their learning and interests center around discovering this purposeful pursuit.
- They also describe an inner connection that brings them peace or confidence.
- Pairing intuitive intelligence with spiritual intelligence can strengthen children's connections and broaden their empathy and creativity.
- Spirituality is a subset of spiritual intelligence. Children can learn spiritual skills like prayer and compassion.
- Spiritual intelligence provides the faith to deal with adversity and a foundation of optimism all children will need in life.
- Intuition is the interpreter of the qualities of spiritual intelligence.
- Intuition is a path into the sacred inner space of spiritual intelligence.
- Children need strategies to find their inner wisdom and access it for their daily affairs. One strategy is to relax, close their eyes, and use their imagination to find answers. Another strategy is to place their hand on their heart, center in the heart, and ask a question. Listening for the heart's answer provides another response besides the logical one.
- Using and dialoging their inner voice of wisdom provides a foundation of strength from which to draw answers and insight.

14

Psychic Talents and Intuitive Intelligence

I like to think of psychic energy as akin to radio waves. Even without the radio on, the air is filled with invisible signals from countless radio stations operating on their various frequencies. All you have to do to receive them is to flick the radio on and tune the dial.

—John Edwards

We've learned in previous chapters that intuitive intelligence is a normal human function from research provided by cardiopsychology and neuro-science, especially brain-mapping. We know that on the higher end of the range of intuitive intelligence are people with exceptional skills, which we call psychic. We use this term because of its popularity. People understand the word *psychic* thanks to televised shows featuring psychics, ghost whisperers, dog whisperers, and mentalists. Other names include paranormal ability or psi. Intuition and extrasensory perception are, however, normal capabilities.

In this chapter we'll discuss intuitive children's psychic talents, needs, and strategies for nurturing their gifts.

Natural Intelligences	Plus Intuitive Intelligence =
Physical Prowess Enhanced by Intuitive Intelligence	
Physical	*Learns by doing, has exceptional kinesthesia, motor skills, sense of timing, and movement with the body.*
Creative, Inspired Intuitive	
Mental-Creative	*Inspired, inventive, creative, follows inner music, ideas, and actions motivated by internal genius. Can daydream, be distracted, learns to focus, and learns through experimentation.*
Empathic Intuitive	
Emotional-Social	*Reads others, feels others, defines self in relation to others. Needs boundaries, emotional management skills, self-identification, and confidence.*
Psychic Intuitive	
Intuitive	*Expanded awareness of the nonphysical worlds or subtle energy fields through receptors in the biochemistry. Exhibits talents of subtle knowing, hearing, seeing, telepathy, and other talents.*
Spiritual Intuitive	
Spiritual	*Intuition serves kids with spiritual intelligence as the doorway and interpreter to connection with inner worlds.*

Intuitive episodes

An intuitive episode is a single occurrence or connection to the inner or nonphysical world. Ethel's story is an example of intuitive episodes.

Ethel, an 83-year old grandmother, who lived by herself, described three separate incidences or psychic episodes in her life. At age 19, she was a married woman living on her husband's family farm. One morning while she was tending her garden, her heart fluttered and fear gripped her. She immediately thought of her husband. She rose from her garden and ran to the barn, fearing the worst. Her husband had fallen from a high ladder and hit his head on a rock, dying instantly. She felt the accident as it was happening. She explained, "I felt his spirit rise up, as if it physically left my own heart chamber."

Ethel would not consider herself a psychic person, but the intuitive episodes in her life were connected to the only two men she deeply loved. During the depression, Ethel found work as a bar maid, and fell in love with the owner of the bar. They married and after 30 years, Ethel had a dream that her second husband told her he was going to die of cancer. She said nothing, just held it close to her heart. Seven years passed before her husband died of lung cancer. She was devastated and grieved heavily. A week after his funeral, Ethel's husband appeared at the foot of her bed one night as she prayed her nightly rosary. He stayed long enough to explain he was happy; he would be there when she passed over, and he would always love her.

Twenty-five years passed before Ethel's death. Ethel never described herself as an intuitive person, and she was positive that her episodes were otherworldly experiences.

Many people have intuitive or psychic episodes and do not consider themselves as being intuitive or having psychic perceptions.

The Harris Poll conducted a survey of 2,455 Americans in 2005 and 2007 about religious and other beliefs. The numbers for people who believe in the paranormal held consistent for two years and showed an upward trend. Psychic experiences are on the rise. People are also more willing to speak about the topic. The beliefs seem to cross all religious groups. The results included:

"Large majorities of the public believe in miracles (79%), heaven (75%), angels (74%), that Jesus is God or the son of God (72%), the resurrection of Jesus (70%), the survival of the soul after death (69%), hell (62%), the devil (62%), and the virgin birth (Jesus born of Mary) (60%).

"Sizeable minorities believe in ghosts (41%), UFOs (35%), witches (31%), astrology (29%), and reincarnation (21%)."[1]

Intuitive episodes like Ethel's can occur for people who have experienced intense emotions such as grief, traumas, or accidents. They occur in dream episodes or when the mind is distracted and able to imagine and daydream. What characterizes intuitive episodes?

- Episodes seem to be unbound by time perceptions. People receive knowledge in the gestalt sense like a déjà vu.

- They are not logical. The experiencer cannot specify how it happened in step-by-step sequence.

- Intuitive episodes occur involuntarily to the perceiver.

Intuitive episodes or psychic incidents may or may not imply that the person is high in intuitive intelligence. Only the person who keeps track of the incidences could make that evaluation.

However, the psychic traits of a child in the highest range of intuitive intelligence are consistently so. Their psychic radar, so to speak, is always available. The constancy of the awareness and consistency of tuning into it are characteristics of psychics.

Psychic talents

On the chart of natural intelligences, we are exploring the intuitive child who has exceptional intuition manifesting as psychic talents.

The psychic talents appear as heightened sensory awareness and feelings as well as the ability to interpret that holistic information. Psychic abilities like those listed below can be acquired skills that one trains to develop. An intuitively gifted child naturally displays one, several, or all of these skills.

Clairvoyance is the ability to see the non-physical world—the ability to see visions, pictures, and energy forms around people, animals, and plants. Your child will use visual words such as see, glimpse, perceive, or notice.

Clairvoyant children describe colors, geometric shapes, lights, beings, eyes, faces, and characteristics that catch their eyes such as hair color, hands, or a piece of clothing. These details can be very important to discern. Such visuals and how the child connects to that world provide your clues for how to support their gifts.

Clairaudience is the ability to hear in the other world, whether music, sound, voice, or telepathic thoughts, and to communicate with others. Children will use words such as *hear, say, listening, understanding, being told,* or repeating exactly what they hear. Parents ask, "What is clairaudient communication like?" The voice of another—angel, ghost, teacher—is different from the child's voice with tenor, emotional quality, and different use of words than they would use. Sometimes, there is even a unique sense of humor or lightheartedness.

Clairsentience is like empathy, the child has the ability to feel another's emotions, sense their moods, even be aware if patterns of behavior of the other. This is the trickiest terrain for psychic children to negotiate because they can internalize those feelings as their own. The child picks up feelings and is able read the energy for content and interpretation. For example, on a recent tour of cathedrals in Europe, Lynn K. enjoyed sitting quietly in churches and absorbing the feelings of its history. She visited church museums and touched crowns, scepters, religious objects, and relics. As she touched each, she understood the story of the object and felt the emotional charge of the object.

Claircognizance is the sense of knowing, like Ethel knowing her husband was gone. Déjà vu, feeling you've seen or done something already, is an example of understanding the whole picture at one time.

A psychic child may show one or several strengths. The only way you will know is to observe what takes place, keeping in mind that the talents are more likely seen at the ages described in the developmental chapter.

Rules of psychic engagement

"Researchers have found that children who are resilient are skillful at creating beneficial relationships with adults, and those relationships in turn contribute to the children's resilience"[2]

In the world of psychic children, parents face the unknown, as do the children. The world becomes known through the eyes and interpretation of the perceiver. There are many families in which the parent and child are psychic, may experience the same vision, ghost, angel, or déjà vu, and can share a "common mind" so to speak. Then there are parents who do not understand their child's visions or worlds. From our years of experience, we have found some common ground to share with you.

- Remain in the present moment when dealing with psychic experiences. Be in the here and now when dealing with phenomena.

- Assume nothing about the experience. Rather, ask questions of the ghost or of the child who has the experience, and expect an answer.

- Have no judgments about the experience because your child will feel it, even if you try to hide it. The younger the child, the more they internalize. The more psychic the child, the more they read your incongruence.

- Be totally honest in your feelings and conversations. Admitting you don't know is okay to do and helping your child find the inner answers is even better.

- Remain centered and calm yourself. Follow the tips for doing so that appear in the next chapter.

- Several parents have asked us to address specific issues that they faced in accepting and working with their child.

Take it in stride

"Caron, do you have a minute?" asked Carol, who was 23 years old and a new mom. Carol had a dream when she was pregnant about her son being a child with special gifts. Her son, Lou, was 18 months old.

"Sure, Carol. What can I help you with?"

"Lou keeps throwing up, and I wondered if you could check in and tell me what's going on?"

"The first thing I see, Carol, is food allergies. He has milk allergies, peanut allergies, and also allergies to fruits. Specifically, I see strawberries and grapes."

"Wow, he's throwing up his milk and peanut butter sandwich right now."

"It looks like you have to stop feeding him that, and perhaps start rotating the foods he likes so he isn't eating the same thing throughout a period of several days."

"But he only likes peanut butter sandwiches and milk."

"What do you mean? Doesn't he drink water? Won't he eat some vegetables, baby foods, a little pasta?"

"No, just what I said. He refuses to eat anything else. So I feed him what he wants."

"Carol, doing that isn't working. The food has made him hypersensitive."

"But he is supposed to be a spiritual child. So when he tells me what he wants, I think he knows best."

"Carol, that's not true. Look, we need to have a longer talk about child rearing and food. Let's schedule an appointment."

In her innocence, Carol believed that because her son was "special," that he would know what his body needed and essentially that he could raise himself. She wanted to support the soul she dreamed about, but hadn't a clue about how to raise a human being.

Maybe all of us have a Carol reflection in our desire to honor our children, talk with them about their gifts, and find way to nurture their dreams. We can honor their souls' purpose as well as help them be phenomenal, successful humans.

Sound familiar? Some of us have been there and done that.

When we tell this story at conferences, people laugh and identify with Carol's innocence. After all, we are new to this psychic stuff when we find our children have unique skills sets that get swept under the rug.

So our first guideline is to **do your homework.**

Our second guideline is to **take it in stride.**

Do your homework

On the blog for intuitive parenting (*intuitiveparenting.wordpress.com*) you may have followed Tara's stories about her psychic son, Caden. This is Tara's story of doing her homework: "I was already aware that Caden had psychic abilities of seeing colors and energetically healing. He talked about colors, seeing his grandpa, and liked to place his hands on family members.

When Caden was 4 years old, I attended a New Age Fair in Nashville where a medium gave me more information about Caden and overwhelmed me. She told me that he had knowledge about the energy matrix (or what some refer to as the grid), and I wondered what that meant. She went on to say that my son had knowledge locked inside of his inner blue print about how the divine energy works and most people on the planet were yet to be made aware of it. Whoa!

How daunting for a parent who was becoming comfortable with her own intuitive abilities and who doesn't have the psychic abilities my son has. At first, I created a flurry for myself. My mind worried endlessly about what I should be doing as his parent to nurture these abilities without a clear understanding of how magnificent this gift could be.

I spent the next few years doing my homework. I researched the Internet for information about what the "matrix" was and what one could energetically do to tap into it. I read as many New Age books as I could find with a metaphysical explanation for energy and how it works. I wondered what Caden was meant to do? How could I nurture these gifts? Would I fail him if I didn't? Would I fail humanity? I asked every spiritually gifted person I came into contact with if they had information about what this could mean and should I "do" anything for him I wasn't already doing?

Finally I learned to watch how Caden tuned into his inner knowing. I realized that he would lead me to what he needed to support his psychic gifts. In the end, there wasn't much I needed to know or do other than to be there to offer him the nurturing support he would need when the energy became too much for him.

I observed his amazing abilities to self-direct his energy by grounding himself naturally with water or in the dirt. I learned techniques like effective breathing to help him calm his nervous system when he couldn't get a handle on his empathic emotions.

Like Carol and her dream, parents can get too much information that creates an overwhelming, stressful environment for everyone. We want to be there for our kids, not realizing that being ourselves is our greatest asset. As parents of intuitively intelligent children, have confidence. It is all right not to know. You can learn and educate yourself. In the end, trust your own intuition! Books and people can help too. As parents, we suggest you:

- Tune into your heart and gut for discernment on actions to take.
- Check in with your common sense also.
- Tune into your child's inner guidance and knowing.
- Observe your children and let them lead you to what they need.
- Breathe!

Working with fears

Caron slept at her mother's house to prepare for her mother coming home from cancer surgery after a week-long stay in the hospital. As she went to bed the first night, Caron felt the house was fearful and imagined how alone her mom must have felt during the last three years since her husband died. Caron was restless, yet managed to meditate, relax, and drift into a light sleep. Within the hour, she felt someone sit on the right side of the bed and touch her knee with a hand. Primal fear gripped her gut and froze her breath. Adrenalin pumped and her heart raced as she sat up in bed quickly. Her first thought was of her father. Yet she felt no familiarity with the energy in the room. Scanning the darkness, she noted no light, no familiar friend, or guide. She chose to not focus on the energy.

Next, Caron turned on the light and followed the trail of fear like a dog follows a scent. As she walked through the house, her intuition felt clearer. She discovered the fear trace was confined to her bedroom and her mother's room, which was across the hall from hers. After calming her own fear, Caron centered herself and filled her heart with the brightest light she could muster. Then she blasted the heart energy like a fireworks display through the room until she felt at peace inside and peace around her.

Our third guideline is **build the strength and light inside for coping with fear.** Trying to protect yourself from the other side dissipates your power and makes you withdraw from the environment. Face it and embrace it with courage, and find inner resilience.

Our fourth guideline is **use ritual with children for a sense of calming.** Prayers, rituals, calling on the angels, and such entities are practices that calm the mind and sometimes help the body feel safe. If a child doesn't feel safe with the use of a ritual, then the child's intuition won't let the mind be tricked or lulled into another focus until the intuitive information is heard and dealt with.

The power of heart light

If you are a psychic or a parent who feels out of balance when dealing with energy situations—ghosts, healing, emotionally draining conversations, readings, or coaching, this one, easy technique can renew your energy and feeling of wholeness. You will stay grounded as well. Imagine a bright sun in your heart center. Turn an imaginary knob to brighten the sun's rays to brilliance. Then breathe deeply and fully to increase and expand the brightness in your heart. Continue breathing for several moments until the light's brightness extends in all directions from your heart center.

Feel a sense of warmth and peace in your body. The inner light is now your beacon and an endless source of energy, renewable by your focus and your breathing. It is easy to restore yourself to balance. For further grounding, imagine sending the light downward through your body, out your feet, and into the earth. This way your inner light can anchor you so you feel more grounded, balanced, and rooted in your daily activities. This imagery strengthens your inner reserves.

Managing fears

We get many questions from parents about children who see and are scared of ghosts. Most parents we hear from are at a loss about what to do. One parent believes the child and one parent does not. The child gets mixed emotional responses. The child wants to sleep with the parents, have the lights turned on, or be in the parent's room. It can become a confusing web. Let's untangle it.

We shared Caron's story of feeling the primal fear in her mother's home to illustrate how fearful children can be when the primal fear hits their gut. Primal fear is the instinctual, survival fear that warns us of life-threatening dangers. Your child's visceral fright causes anxiety symptoms. Calming them is the priority before acting on the issue of ghosts.

Step one is to calm yourself. Even if you are initially uncomfortable or scared to death yourself, be the leader. Move ahead to support your child physically, emotionally, and mentally through their fear. As parents, we must be able to shift our moods and respond from strength.

1. If a child claims to see a ghost, we accept that they believe they see one. Any debate about the reality of what they see is a moot point until after the episode has passed. When our children ask for help, we help.

2. If you, the parent, are scared, then say so and move ahead to help your child. Telling a child to try an exercise on her own because you don't want to go into their room is not helpful. One of you has to be the leader.

3. Whatever exercise you use, do it with your child. Or, show her, and then let the child practice until you see a sense of ease in using it. Some rituals that help a child focus on affirming action if frightened by ghosts have different goals:

    -   Lighting a candle and using the light to clear away the ghost.

    -   Touching the ghost in friendship, hand to hand, and one of two things will happen. The ghost disappears or the child makes a friend, and learns why the ghost is there and what it wants.

    -   Saying no to the ghost and demanding the ghost leave, and waiting until it does. Close the doorway. Ask your child to see a door, describe it, and then close it after the ghost with his or her own hand.

    -   If ghosts can come, then so can angels. Call on angels and wait until your child can see them. Ask the angels for help and move ahead—talk with them, ask questions, and get answers.

    -   Don't treat the ghosts and other worldly phenomena as an untouchable space. You can touch it. Choose interaction. Be proactive!

Taking actions such as these provides an immediate remedy to calm a fearful child or distressed situation. However, they don't begin to reveal the whole picture of a psychic child's abilities. In other words, defensive rituals may help in an instance and do nothing to nurture your child's gift for the long run. Your child may also need help in learning not to be afraid or how to manage fear-based states. For example, surrounding ourselves with white light uses the imagination and can be a useful mental defense for the moment. Mental defenses help to calm the panic and restore a child to confidence, even if short-lived.

In the long run, however, you are telling your child that there are bogie men, ghosts, and ghouls "out there in some invisible world," and they need protection from them. Instead, we invite you to see a bigger picture of the nonphysical world and the interrelationship with physical world. They are both "real," and you can teach your child to feel safe in them.

Acupressure points for calming

With your thumbs or two fingers, touch the acupuncture points at the temples, placing two fingers at the end of each brow. Press gently for three seconds and lift. Then repeat several more times until you feel more relaxed. Press gently as tissue is delicate. Other calming points are at the top of either brown line, starting at the top of the brow and moving inward toward the nose. Stop at the edge of the brow. These are sensitive and delicate points also, and when you bring your fingers to touch them gently for five seconds, do so with compassion or love. Convey respect for your child and for their situation.

If your child were a musical prodigy, you would find a teacher or mentor to nurture the gift. Why not do the same for a gifted psychic child? If your daughter is going to a new school, you educate yourselves. You visit the school, find out who the teachers, are and help her with a new schedule. We need to do the same for psychic children. Read ghost stories, watch age-appropriate movies, and help quiet your child's fears. It can also help you with any fears you may have.

Then, make it a game to talk to the ghosts, get their descriptions, and draw pictures. Treat it as an adventure and keep a ghost diary. The whole point of learning together is to accept your child as normal; and that her gifts are the norm for your family. Your child's interest will show you how much attention to devote to the topic of ghosts. Trust both of you and have some fun!

Benji's friend

Six-year-old Benji, an empathic psychic, told his mom about a friend who was a ghost who visited him around bedtime. According to Benji, the ghost was another child about his age and Benji called him Frank. At first mom didn't think much about it, as she knew kids had invisible friends. A little later, Benji said that Frank wanted to play in his room at bedtime. Mom listened without offering advice as Benji was reporting, not asking for help.

One evening when Benji's mom was turning in, she checked in on him because his bedroom light was still on. Benji was crying softly, and explained that he'd been discussing Frank's situation with him. Frank had shared with Benji through telepathy that he was sad. What Frank remembered was that his parents were killed in a car, and he didn't know where they were. He found an empathic human who recognized him and he felt good in Benji's house. Could he stay there and maybe live with the family and be Benji's brother?

Benji's mom suggested that a psychic might guide Frank to his parents, or better yet, Benji could help by calling on his angels or Frank's angels. Then a deeper level of the psychic connection came through.

Because Benji's parents were divorced, he understood Frank's pain of loss and felt sorry for him. Benji, feeling deep empathy, was inclined not to send Frank away because he didn't want him to be lonely. Benji's mom was more inclined to shut out the whole ghost situation somehow as it was absorbing her son's energetic focus. However she displayed the kindest gift of patience. She listened and she waited. When Benji was ready to let Frank go more than a month later, mom and he created a ritual by opening a doorway of light and encouraging Frank to say goodbye and walk through it.

Heartwise virtues in the psychic world

Virtues from the heart are markers of excellence. When we find them as part of an intuitive child's inborn strength, we can expect their inner motivation to mobilize their journey. We can also cultivate virtues in children by modeling our ethics and including them in actions, which demonstrate virtues. For example, patient listening is a virtue in a fast-paced life. A child who is heard doesn't have a need to gain attention in negative ways.

Virtues give strength and enhance, rather than drain energy. They sustain one through adversity, and we still feel children with high intuitive intelligence have challenges in this society that requires their utmost confidence. Two virtues that we encourage are being ordinary, which is authenticity, as well as courage.

1. **Being Ordinary**—Of as much concern to a parent and a psychic child about handling the nonphysical world is handling the ordinary world. Our soulful and purposeful children must successfully negotiate family, peers, and school with optimism and self-confidence. Without giving our children labels for how they learn or labels for their talents, we allow our children the privilege of not having to live up to anyone else. We empower their freedom to be authentic!

2. **Courage to face fear**—False guidance is rooted in fear. The underlying assumption is that the world is unsafe and that you are not secure, so the guidance will be aimed at increasing your degree of control. Genuine intuitive guidance comes from a place of love and the assumption that you are perfectly safe and secure as you are, so instead of trying to gain control, the focus is on expressing your true self and trusting your connection to the nonphysical worlds.

3. **Commitments to helping others**—Studies reveal that higher survival rates in HIV-infected men and women were positively associated with optimism and being helpful to others. When we reach beyond ourselves and fill our heart with gratitude, the psychic child may experience inner peace.

4. Mindfulness—our children's ability to be aware of the present—their feelings, their environment, their intuitive nudges. Awareness helps them translate feelings and thoughts into actions or choices.

• • •

In the book, *Authoritative Communities, The Scientific Case for Nurturing the Whole Child* (Springer, 2008) the author, Kathleen Kline makes it clear that our children are born to attach to their primary caregiver. Think of it as a biological imperative, which is the essential foundation for moral meaning. The human child is talked into talking, loved into loving, and moved to fear or strength through the positive connections of those in his world. Coping mechanisms derive from the cultivation of virtues such as gratitude, forgiveness, patience, and hope. Although children are born with innate temperaments as discussed in Chapter 1, our nurturing aspect shapes the qualities and character of the psychic child.

Chapter Review

- An intuitive episode or a psychic incident is a one-time event, not implying the person is psychic consistently.
- According to a Harris Poll, the numbers of people who believe in the paranormal is rising and crosses all religious groups.
- The constancy of the awareness and consistency of tuning into the other worlds are characteristics of psychics, persons high in natural intuitive intelligence.
- Psychic talents include the clairvoyance, clairaudience, clairsentience, and knowing.
- Rules of psychic engagement include being in the present moment, be open, honest, and without judgment.
- Guidelines for parents of psychic children include take it in stride, do your homework, build a powerbase of light inside for working with fears, and use ritual with children for calming and centering.
- Virtues from the heart are markers of excellence. When we find them as part of an intuitive child's inborn strength, we can expect their inner motivation to mobilize their journey.

15

Empowerment and Intuition

The answers to our questions cannot come from the incomplete consciousness of the intellect but from a deeper revelation that may be born from our instincts, a new mythology of the whole of life as a divine unity. There is, in this new myth, no essential distinction between transcendent and immanent life; as the mystics have always told us, the distinction and the dualism are in our distorted perception of reality. The divine is what we are.

—Anne Baring, *The Spirit of Science*

Empowering great choices and voices

In previous chapters, we've discussed intuitive children being proactive and feeling confident. When confidence is coupled with competence or skills, intuitive parents and children have strong foundations for empowerment—facing the emotional and sensory bombardment in their environments and making good choices for their emotional and mental health. As soon as some intuitive children start school or make shifts to new school settings, parents see reactive behaviors. These are a sample of complaints that we've heard from concerned parents whose children were making school transitions:

- "Chris has this deep sadness when he comes home from kindergarten. He comes home and crashes in front of the television, which we haven't allowed until now because he needs to zone out. He says he feels sad for two children in his class who get picked on."

- "Liz started junior high this week, and came home nauseated her first three days of school. She said she had a tummy ache. We made her go back to school and on the fourth morning, she protested. Her mom and I could have forced her, but that wasn't the answer. Finally she confessed that a gang of girls at her school started picking on her and other newbies in the locker room. We can't make her go back to that."

- "Jason came to live with me, his dad, and his new step mom and sister. I explained that we couldn't afford a private high school as he had previously attended, and he said that public school was all right. He lasted about two weeks, and came home in tears. His teacher in freshman English chewed the class out because she said everyone flunked their tests and then she threw them in the trash. Jason pulled his test out of the trash and asked her to grade it. Even though he aced the test, the teacher refused to treat him "special." We couldn't get him transferred to another class, and this sensitive, gifted child was suffering. We found a private school, and we found a way to pay for it."

The stories illustrate how intuitive children with sensitivities are easily overwhelmed by environmental overload. The overload can be loud sounds, lights, emotional discord, mental overload, or intuitive bombardment. In her book, *The Highly Sensitive Child, Helping Our Children Thrive When the World Overwhelms Them* (2002), author Elaine Aron shares how highly sensitive persons notice more in their environment and reflect on decisions deeply before acting. Aron says, "Mainly, their brains process information more thoroughly…sensitive children and adults have faster reflexes; are more affected by pain, medications, and stimulants; and have a more reactive immune system and more allergies. In this sense, their entire body is designed to detect and understand more precisely whatever comes in."[1]

Sometimes, as parents of intuitives, we feel caught in the conundrum of confusion in helping our children build resilience and make decisions on the spot about how to handle a bully, communicate with a negative teacher, or be caring with a friend who hurts. In other words, how do we empower our children to speak up and make good choices? Many intuitive adults have withdrawn from social structures, and some empathic children are called introverted when they are only pulling back from "overload."

Empowerment is an experience of confidence! Empowering moments happen when a child feels success inside himself or develops solutions to an issue in which he finds success.

Empowered choices and actions

Phyllis K. Peterson, author of Healing the Wounded Soul, *shares this story in her speech, "Empowering Our Daughters." Nine-year-old Anisa Kintz created a conference, "Calling all Colors" to open people's eyes to racism in the educational system. Two hundred people participated, and the President of the United States awarded Anisa the Thousand Points of Light award.*

Reader's Digest *(June 2008) featured an article about an empowered group of students and their teacher, Patty Hall, who was ready to retire from teaching when she got an e-mail. Christopher Mutuku was Ms. Hall's driver on her trips to Kenya, and his e-mail asked for her help in raising funds to build a dam of sand. The cost would be about $7,000. Within six months, Hall's students raised $12,000. The project, H2O for Life, has now spread to 14 other schools that now raise money to bring clean water to African communities.*

Whether as individuals or as a group, students who are empowered can achieve global missions and make a difference in the others' lives. Their voices were heard. They took action. Their parents supported them and their efforts were appreciated and acknowledged.

Our children's intutive gifts, whether creative, empathic, psychic, artistic, or entrepreneurial are the doorways for their self-expression and empowered actions. Intuitive kids need your support, whether or not you are an intutive parent. Because intuitive kids can feel each time you are not sincere, caring, or congruent in your messages, we have to get our acts together. The primary actions for parents of intuitive children are:

1. Respecting—offer positive regard for an intuitive's talents or activities.
2. Hearing—listen to all that someone has to say.
3. Acknowledging—accepting, noticing, validating.
4. Valuing—to consider their worth, importance, and contribution.
5. Appreciating—to be grateful for their unique contribution or mission.
6. Supporting—to give help, provide comfort, and emotional support.

These six actions of love buffer children from the overflow of creativity that results in being called on the carpet, empathy that results in meltdown or psychic skills that frighten the psychic child. To feel empowered in the use of their gifts, these children need the extra insulation.

Kellie's empowerment

Kellie found empowerment through her empathic connection to whales in her childhood. She grew into adolescence and read about the sonar testing programs being used by the United States Navy in marine mammal sanctuaries. The result has been beached whales and calves. Kellie felt deep heart pain, and after much discussion with her parents, was able to transform her pain into action. Her sense of justice carried her into the environmental movement to halt the use of sonar testing by supporting the filing of lawsuits and educating others in her community.

Empowered children develop trust in their intuition. They also acquire a form of self-discipline, which can

- put feet on their creativity.
- give words to their visions.
- transform negative emotion into positive action.
- inspire pro-activity.
- find humor or the silver lining in any situation.

In summary then, children gain empowerment by seeing the effectiveness of their personal beliefs, intuitions, and actions, all of which start with parent-child interactions.

Parenting phrases to soothe and support

- *You're great.*
- *I'm so glad you are here.*
- *Welcome to my life.*
- *I am glad that you are my child.*
- *You can handle it. You are resilient.*
- *Go for it.*
- *Your eyes shine today. You must be happy.*
- *Your eyes and mouth are smiling.*
- *We are having a good time, aren't we?*
- *Go ahead and ask questions. Your mind wants an answer.*
- *Speak up. Your opinion is important here.*
- *You matter. You make a difference.*

Transfer of Power

Although we make every decision for our infants, we then eventually transfer decision-making power to our children through the choices we encourage children to make. This "transfer of power" happens in two stages:

1. Belief stage: Through observation and through trial and error, parents learn to trust in the child's ability to make choices. For example, when preteens are given a 10 p.m. curfew, do they stretch out the rules and come in later and later? Or, do they consistently return home at the agreed-upon time? Parents observe these behaviors and form their beliefs about their child's ability to make choices.

When a 6-year-old empath has to vent emotion after coming home from school, what is his choice for *how* to vent emotion? Do you step into this emotional moment and help her choose to talk it through, take a walk, cry and hug a pillow, or go to the art corner and paint, color, or draw the expression? If your child can choose their venue for emotional outlet, are they accurate? Does the solution work? Then, can you trust their choices?

Rose is 10 and has a highly gifted mind that loves to write. She has written a booklet and wants to publish copies from the family computer to sell to neighbors. Her parents ask themselves the following questions to find out how Rose might need support. Is she able to plan each step of the publishing process? How she will sell the booklets? Do they support the entrepreneurial endeavor? Do they think she is old enough to complete the tasks and interact well with the neighbors?

These are real-life scenarios from intuitive children whose gifts vary from creative inspiration to deep feeling. Intuitive children frequently start making choices earlier than other children as they experience more kinesthetic clues. The timing of a choice may feel right to an intuitive before a cognitive child gathers enough information for the decision.

Ten-year-old Jean was adamant that she have a birthday in honor of her best friend, Caroline. Her parents were inclined not to have the party, but were swept along in Jean's insistence and planning until they sat back to watch their daughter take charge. Jean set the date, passed out invitations to their mutual friends, bought and wrapped Caroline's gift, designed games, and decorated the family's den for a Saturday afternoon party. Jean acted on her mission, and its immediacy and her diligence surprised them as well as Caroline's parents.

The successful party went off without a hitch. The 20 10-year olds ate and played games and watched a movie, prolonging the party into the early evening hours. Afterward, Jean thanked her parents profusely and said she knew it was so very important to have the party. Her parents asked why and Jean could only say, "I knew it had to happen now."

Within six months, Caroline developed a cancer and missed birthday parties for several years while in medical treatment, but she spoke of her 10th year as her best year. Jean knew.

2. Allowing stage: Parents allow and encourage their children to make certain decisions in this stage of empowering. Jean's parents allowed her to move ahead with the party because of insistence and enthusiasm, which was unusual for a 10-year-old, but not an intuitive 10-year-old who is confident in her abilities. They transferred the decision-making skills to Jean and observed her progress.

Jason is a 13-year-old creative intuitive with much inspiration to try new activities for the pure pleasure of the experience. His family has learned that he has a lot of crazy ideas like biking across the country or raising funds for a homeless shelter. His parents honored his inspiration to raise money for the shelter, but did not allow plans for a bike-a-thon.

Instead, Jason suggested he plan his family's annual summer vacation, to which his parents agreed. For him, planning a trip to see dinosaur artifacts was the first step, and he chose The Museum of the Rockies in Bozeman, Montana, for his family's vacation. He wrote out transportation options and even listed travel experiences for his parents. Jason was very thoughtful and empathic about choosing what he felt his parents would enjoy. Jason taught his younger brother to close his eyes, and imagine being next to a dinosaur and listening to what life was like millions of years ago in Montana.

Transferring power, then, is about encouraging belief in one's power of choice and positive action. Such beliefs and actions encourage their esteem.

Empowerment and esteem

By the time children are in school, they have translated their esteem into values that they've internalized. A child filters every decision through his value system. If a child values herself, she has a strong sense of who she is, and chooses healthy social interactions. She likely is empathic and sees another's point of view. If a child does not value herself, the others' opinions, actions, and requests of her easily influence her.

As parents, we continue to help intuitive children clarify their values and strengthen their self-esteem through clear communication. Here are principles to help children think and clarify what is important to them when faced with a challenge:

- Identify the problem.
- Think through options.
- Identify consequences.
- Listen in silence without trying to fix.
- Assert themselves if they need to do this.
- Appreciate their interests and efforts.

As children grow older, they gain esteem through accomplishment, just as adults do. They value their effort and time invested in a project or an act of kindness.

Encourage intuitive strength

- *Be the coach. Encourage a creative to move through a project that seems boring, hard, or intense for them. Help them focus and finish.*

- *Be the cheerleader. If we know they can do it and they are stuck, ask them to try another way. Take a break and come back with fresh eyes. Or, ask questions to help them think through the situation. Focus and finish.*

- *Be the leader. Experience new adventures with them. Plan and produce.*

- *Be the inviter. Challenge them and stretch their abilities within safety limits. Plan and produce.*

- *Be the optimist. Help them cope with defeat. Feel and be real.*

- *Be the realist. Help them deal with situations realistically. Feel and be real.*

- *Be a parent with heart. Teach them empathy. Be aware and take care.*

- *Be an example of service. Involve them in projects that feel good to their hearts. Be aware and take care.*

Support for the spiritual intuitive

Spiritual empowerment comes from a child's personal values and sense of worth. How do we encourage the passion and joy for living, that sense of a child's inner fire? When children connect to their inner selves, it becomes the intrinsic drive for their productivity and relationships. Children connected to their inner spirits are curious and exploratory and have minds of their own. Though such children may need boundaries and structures, they may resist restrictions until you help them understand *why* they need such boundaries.

Remember the spiritual intuitive needs the question why and its answer. We believe that cognitive Q and A connects the inner resilience and the outer action.

Parenting coach and trainer, Rebecca Woulfe, has these suggestions:

1. "Use language and images that are in line with your family values. Give children the understanding that they are loved and supported by something bigger than they are. For some families it may be God, or angels, or spirit animals. Whatever is appropriate for you and your family, let them know that they are loved and supported just the way they are. Let them know that they are deserving and worthy of this love and support.

2. Model your own spiritual practices. If you hide your own spiritual beliefs to give your children free choice as an adult, you are asking a seed to grow without water or light. Share your beliefs. When you do, you give your child the rain, the sunlight, and the rich soil for them to blossom into a beautiful flower."[2]

The call of the spirit cuts through the complexities of all our strategies and shows the true nature of love and happiness. Our spirit affirms that which is essential and eternal. The spirit does not directly produce emotions or feelings, but relates to our attitudes. We must ultimately learn to live in harmony with the world that surrounds and sustains us.

In this sense, true spirituality deals consciously with life's ultimate meaning, and affirms its sanctity and unconditional worthiness. Compassion, love, hope, forgiveness, and faith are foundations of our physical and emotional life. These concepts are essential and must be conscientiously nourished.

Hope is a necessary spiritual quality for a healthy emotional life. Hope is not "wishful thinking" nor is it based on unrealistic goals. Hope shows the deepest wishes and motivations of life itself. Hope is the positive response to crisis and challenge, creating realistic and positive expectations. Instilling hope in your child shows that you together have the natural ability to overcome any problem as it might occur. Trusting in this inborn spiritual capacity for resolution and change is the first major step in the solution.

Honoring your child's strengths

When you identify your children's areas of strength, it helps them develop confidence in themselves. Try this exercise and see for yourself. Ask your children to develop their own list of positive personal qualities, such as:

- *A warm sense of humor.*
- *A strong ability to create with their hands.*
- *Helpfulness to others.*
- *Courage in difficult situations.*
- *An ability to recognize fear and move through it anyway.*

Next, have them list the positive qualities of each family member. This encourages them to look for and name good characteristics in others. More than that, they feel connected with people. And the very act of making a list is, in itself, empowering.

Empowerment demands that we interact with our children and model the use and trust of intuition. Empowerment results when children experience natural consequences of their choices. Then they review their mistakes and take accountability for their learning. We coach their empowerment by asking open-ended questions to stimulate choices: What did you learn? How would you do it differently? Can you list the choices you might make that are different for next time this happens? What other options did you have? What resources might you need? What do you think is possible in that situation? How will you handle this mistake? What might be the longer-term effects? What else might affect the outcome?

Chapter Review

- When confidence is coupled with competence or skills, intuitive parents and children have strong foundations for empowerment— facing the emotional and sensory bombardment within their environments and making good choices for their emotional and mental health.

- Empowerment is an experience of confidence! Empowering moments happen when a child has felt success inside him or developed solutions to an issue in which he found success.

- Our children's intutive gifts, whether creative, empathic, psychic, artistic, or entrepreneurial are the doorways for their self-expression and empowered actions.

- Children achieve empowerment by experiencing confidence through their personal beliefs, intuitions, and actions, all of which start with parent-child interactions.

- Transferring power, then, is about encouraging belief in one's power of choice and positive action. Such beliefs and actions encourage their esteem.

- Spiritual empowerment comes from a child's personal values and sense of worth.

- Though spiritual children may need boundaries and structures, they may resist restrictions until you help them understand *why* they need such boundaries.

- In this sense, true spirituality deals consciously with life's ultimate meaning, and affirms its sanctity and unconditional worthiness.

- Compassion, love, hope, forgiveness, and faith are foundations of our physical and emotional life.

16

Mental Health and Intuition

The thirteenth principle is known as the sixth sense through which Infinite Intelligence may, and will, communicate voluntarily, without any effort from, or demands by the individual.

—Napoleon Hill

Empowerment and support of children's intuitive gifts cause parents to embark on asking questions and finding answers, especially when confronted by situations in which intuitive children are outside the box and nonconforming. This chapter addresses several of these issues, which we find common in families with intuitive children. Also, Judith Orloff, MD, has graciously contributed her intuitive story and advice.

Judith Orloff, MD, shares

At an early age, Judith Orloff, MD, had intuitive talents that were not supported by her family members even though she came from a long line of intuitives. Dr. Orloff (*www.drjudithorloff.com*), a psychiatrist and intuition expert, is the author of *Emotional Freedom: Liberate Yourself From Negative Emotions* and *Transform Your Life* (Harmony Books, 2009). Her other bestsellers are *Positive Energy, Intuitive Healing*, and *Second Sight*. Dr. Orloff synthesizes the pearls of traditional medicine with cutting edge knowledge of intuition, energy, and spirituality. She passionately believes that the future of medicine involves integrating all this wisdom to achieve emotional freedom and total wellness. She is an Assistant Clinical Professor of Psychiatry at UCLA and has been featured on *The Today, Show*, CNN, and in *Oprah Magazine* and *USA Today*.

Intuition runs in families

Dr. Orloff shares her story that she chronicles in her book *Second Sight*:

I come from a long line of intuitives, which includes my grandmother, mother, cousin, and aunts—the whole female side of my family on my mother's side. Intuition can be passed down in families, definitely. What kind of intuitive gifts a person might have runs more according to their temperament, although there's a lot of modeling that goes on. For example, if the mother has visions, then the daughter may learn to have visions and dreams.

The advice that I would give intuitive parents who know that their children are also intuitive is to help them be comfortable in their own skins—to model the intuition in a seamless way. Don't make too big a deal out of it. The point is for you and your children to be comfortable. When you see a mother who trusts her gut feelings, that's a powerful message to the daughter or son.

Where I've seen parents go wrong if they are intuitive or psychic is they get overzealous. They try and force intuition on their children, and then the children rebel. Psychic moms and dads can be intrusive, where they're always getting these psychic hits about their child everywhere they go, and the child feels suffocated. The point is that every intuitive should be comfortable in their own skin.

When I was young and would have intuitions about my parents' friends, they would always say to me, 'How can you say that? You don't even know somebody.' Oftentimes intuitive children have these hits about people: whether they can trust them; whether they can't trust them; whether they want to move toward them or move away from them; whether they're scared of them; or whether they're drawn to them. Children have these kinds of intuitions about people that need to be factored into the situation of the family. Sometimes children's intuitive hits may be accurate, sometimes they aren't. Parents need to honor and listen to the child's voice, not dismiss it like my parents did.

My parents said, 'You don't even know somebody.'" When you have intuition, you don't need to know somebody completely to get a sense of him or her. You just sense it. So encourage children to express their intuitions. I'm a big believer in encouraging children to talk about whatever dreams they had around the breakfast table. Parents can listen to the dreams, because intuition comes through dreaming powerfully. Sometimes children have gut feelings about people or situations. Honor them; parents can encourage children to share these kinds of takes on people, and have them be factored into the family instead of dismissed. Parents listen without judging, being able to encourage children to express themselves creatively, intuitively, and directionally, every which way.

Intuitive health versus mental health

Dr. Orloff continues:

When a parent wants to know whether their child is intuitive or has a mental health problem, I distinguish the difference. There's a big difference between psychosis and intuition. For example, if you have a psychotic voice, it comes through and says demeaning things like to hurt yourself or somebody else. It will tell you your food is poisoned. It will have very negative comments about you. Intuitive voices never do that.

Intuitive voices are supportive and kind, maybe with a positive direction in the person's life or their dreams? If the child is psychotic and the child is having a psychotic episode, then that has nothing to do with intuition. It has to do with biochemical imbalance. There's a huge difference.

Teens and Intuition

I've seen, through the years, families, young children, and teens. Before puberty, children are often open to intuition because society hasn't had a chance to shut it off or squash it yet. But when somebody goes through the teenage years, there's more pressure to conform. The intellect starts getting more developed, and then that overpowers the intuition unfortunately. Teenagers sometimes forget they even had intuition. Adults sometimes forget they had it as children. They could have had very profound intuitions as children, but the intellect becomes so strong that they lose track of it, and they lose track of that part of themselves.

A lot of teenagers don't want to have anything to do with intuition. They just want to get along with their friends and fit in. So one shouldn't force intuition on a teenager. However, if a teenager wanted to develop it, then it's very good to teach the teenager to meditate. A three-minute meditation where they can get quiet, be still, and listen to their inner voice is a good start. In quiet, they can see if it is accurate. Once you do, that's kind of exciting. So teenagers would like that. They can go through a period where they can test themselves. Get their guidance, follow it, and trust it.

When parents wonder whether or not they should encourage their teen's intuition, I would say you have to ask the teenager. If the teenager wants to develop it, then you help them. If it isn't something they want to develop, you can tell them you think it's very useful and maybe at a future time they would like to develop it.

However, if somebody is depressed and is receiving treatment for depression, the medication sometimes can numb your intuition and that can separate yourself from your inner voice. So it's important to treat whatever psychological factors or biological factors are contributing to the depression, so that a person can get back to center and feel better mentally. That can help a person just click back in with their intuition.

On the other hand, sometimes teenagers can get depressed because they lose touch with their intuition. That's what happened, in a sense, to me when I was a child and running from my intuitions. I couldn't bear them as a child. They would just overwhelm me too much, and I got involved with drugs and alcohol in my teen years to try and squash my intuitions.

It helped in that I didn't have to have premonitions anymore, or sense other people's energy. I was able to go to shopping malls with my friends without getting overwhelmed by the energy there. It helped. But it didn't help in terms of me developing my intuition.

I had this extreme car accident when I was 16 years old, where I went over a cliff in a car. After that, my parents forced me to see a psychiatrist. Through the help of the psychiatrist, who was able to see that a lot of my anger and depression was about running from my intuitive self, and that for me to be healthy and whole, I had to embrace the intuitions I had as a child. At that point, that angel of a man helped me to come to terms with my intuition. Then he sent me, a teenager, to see Dr. Thelma Moss, who is a parapsychologist at UCLA. She invited me to work as a volunteer in her lab.

That point was the first time in my life I ever had support for intuition.

An empath like me is essentially a sponge. Children and teenagers can be empaths. So they can take on the emotional energy of other people. What I would feel was that I was fine before I went into a mall, and I'd leave feeling exhausted, depressed, and anxious, with some ache or pain I didn't have before. When I went in the mall, I felt bombarded by not only smells and voices and senses and visually, but also, I got overwhelmed by sensing other people. I sensed their emotions or what they were feeling, or just the energy they had. It would exhaust me and deplete me so I wouldn't want to go anymore. Specifically, I got stomach cramps, more in my solar plexus, and I'd be hit with tiredness and anxiety. I was so overwhelmed I couldn't wait to get back home and be quiet. At that time, I took drugs to desensitize.

Now, I am just fierce about my energy management, because I schedule myself to be with people. I love being with people, but then I always have to go home and replenish alone. I spend a lot of time in nature. I spend a lot of time meditating to bring myself back to center. I've also found that when I work on my own personal issues, emotional issues, if I clear them, the less likely I absorb energy from other people.

For a teenager today, it's just as important to set boundaries and say enough is enough. If I'm an empath and if I'm tired when I get overwhelmed by people, the parents can really help the teenager be okay with going home and sitting quietly, or walking in a garden, or whatever they want to do to ground themselves. Teens must know they're not weird or strange when this happens. Parents can help them understand that some people have the sensitivity, and it's a great gift.

You have to tell them it's a great gift because it helps them to develop compassion, but they have to honor it in themselves throughout their life so that they don't get exhausted or irritable or emotionally upset from it.

From the beginning, teens and children with intuition have to learn how to take care of themselves and realize it's a form of great sensitivity that has its pluses and minuses. It's a gift. When you have that sensitivity, you have to take care of your energy. That's all there is to it, and that's a good thing.

It's a form of self-care to teach teens how to set boundaries and limits. They have to know how great it is to be able to say no to somebody if they don't feel like going out. They might need to stay home and replenish, to say no and to set boundaries if things don't feel good, to learn how to find a safe place where they can replenish their energy and all that. It's a very useful education early on.

Emotional environments and intuition

Emotional environments can affect an empath or sensitive intuitive child. They take it much harder, because they take on the energy of the parents and it's frightening to see a parent out of control or to feel whatever depression or anxiety is underneath the alcoholism. So the child takes that on themselves, and either feels like they're to blame, or tries to take away the negative energy of the parent, therefore using his/her own body as a vehicle to do that, to suck up all the negative energy. So that's not helpful at all. That could really hurt a child.

Parents who are depressed or angry and are getting help for it are beautiful role models for children, because all parents will have emotional issues that come up. But the parents that are rage-aholics, or the ones that are depressed, but are not getting help for it, can hurt the child.

When a child sees a parent getting help and getting better, that's really wonderful.

Being grounded

The term grounding *means to have both feet on the ground and to feel stable, not flighty, airy-fairy, dizzy, pulled, pushed, or influenced by another person's energy. John is 16 and reports that he feels spaced out in school in his junior year. To John, spaced out means distracted and not able to pay attention when sitting in his different classes. When he leaves school and returns home, John feels normal again.*

John's parents asked him to keep a time diary of when he felt this way. This pattern emerged after third period—around 10:30 to 11:00 a.m., John spaced out. A doctor tested John for hypoglycemia, allergies, and diabetes, and found him to be in top health.

John decided to use his clairvoyance to scan his body for energy imbalances. He closed his eyes, and with inner eyes, started at the top of his head and moved down through his body to his intestines. He sensed that he needed protein instead of a carbohydrate breakfast. In addition, his body wanted to be grounded through movement or exercise.

Through his school counselor, John rearranged his schedule with physical education at third period and changed his eating habits. John could have searched outside of himself and consulted more medical doctors, but he already had his answers, and listening to his intuition, using his talent, kept him in optimal health.

Nothing is more helpful for intuitive teens than a form of physical discipline or exercise! Swimming classes, calisthenics, yoga, martial arts, running, walking, dancing—these will help teens to feel more confident, strong, and in control. All psychic power and intuitive sensing need grounding through the body.

Traits that might disturb non-intuitive people

All of us adhere to medical, educational, and therapeutic models that value a normative scale of attributes, whether in health, ability to learn or ability to negotiate society and appear sane. These standards are necessary for the treatment of true illness and biochemical imbalances.

However when there is no room for what seems to be "out of the box" thinking and behaving, intuitive gut reactions, or psychic ability, then someone may question your intuitive child's skills, reason, and behavior. P.M.H. Atwater, LHD, author of *Beyond the Indigo Children*, describes these behaviors as, "supersensitive, confident, highly intelligent, unusually creative, nonconformist, extraordinarily psychic and spiritually aware, impatient, empathic, able to heal or aid others in significant ways, abstracting at young ages, spatial learners, great at problem-solving."[1]

Psychic or psychosis

Recently, we received a request for help for seven-year-old Lauren who screamed in her second-grade classroom that the ghost she saw wanted to kill her. Lauren's parents considered her psychic in that she had always seen ghosts, had imaginary playmates, and reported her dead grandfather's presence around the family now and then. To them, this was normal for Lauren.

Now see Lauren through her teacher's eyes. A little girl disrupts the classroom by jumping out of her seat and screaming, "He's going to kill me." The teacher settles Lauren down, takes her out into the hallway, and asks for an explanation. Lauren explained her friendly ghost had turned mean. The teacher would judge her as delusional or hallucinating and confusing realities.

The school nurse calls an ambulance, and little Lauren is taken to the psychiatric hospital where she is medicated to stop the hallucinations. This was an appropriate response on the part of the school. On the other hand, the parents feel they were supporting their child's creative imagination. They understand that Lauren does not meet the criteria for a diagnosis of having a psychosis: no personal history of poor social adjustment or inability to make friends; no incoherence or disorganization of psychological functions, no aggressive and manipulative actions; no basic mistrust of the world and people; no harmful or destructive behavior.

The one symptom that doctors will explore is hallucinations with voices of unpleasant content. Why did Lauren's friendly imaginary ghost scare her and suddenly announce a murderous intention?

You may face such issues if you have an intuitive, psychic child, and this is why you must inform yourself of all aspect of this intuitive talent. We receive more and more reports of children who have access to the non-physical world. Why some see angels and others see ghosts has to do with the inner workings of the child's psyche and the child's environment. One issue of parental confusion is preschoolers who see ghosts at night and those who awaken at night in terror.

Night terrors

Overly sensitive children may be prone to night terrors. Night terrors are when a person wakes up feeling terrified, frightened, screaming, or groaning, and has difficulty being awakened. Most prone to night terrors are preschoolers, and now and then, pubescents. These episodes usually occur between one to two hours into a sleep cycle, and the episode itself can last 15 to 30 minutes. The events usually subside by themselves, and some medical research offers hope for parents of children who experience this frequently.

To offset a night terror, parents can awaken the child 15 to 20 minutes before the event normally occurs. This breaks the brain wave cycle, and returning them to sleep seems to break the terror cycle. Don't confuse these natural childhood events with anything psychic, scary, or ghouly.

There are contributing factors to night terrors and they fall along the line of what contributes to stressing the nervous system:

- Change in routine.
- Lack of sleep, such as a nap during the day.
- Eating two hours before bedtime from foods that exacerbate nerves. Those foods include sugars, excitotoxins, and allergic foods such as peanut butter or chocolate.
- Disturbances in the emotional environments such as arguments or substances.
- Family stressors such as divorce.

Being fierce about boundaries for empaths

In Dr. Orloff's interview, she spoke of being fierce about discipline for empaths. We use the term *discipline* to mean that you train your empathic child or teen in activities that build internal strength and discernment. The end results of these activities are established rituals to:

- **Be aware of triggers** that cause meltdowns or depression or moodiness. This may require a diary, reviewing the event and putting it into words or pictures.
- **Discern identity:** These are my feelings, and those are her feelings. I use these activities or exercises (breathing, walking, moving, stretching) for managing my feelings.
- **Discern when to take action:** Because an empath has a gift does not mean they have to fix situations or make people better. Because they feel does NOT mean they are responsible for or having to act on that feeling.
- **Learn that their job** is to be aware and take care of themselves. They know that sugar causes moodiness, not to play with a friend who doesn't feel right to them, say no to an event that doesn't settle well in the gut and not be fixated on a strange feeling without understanding why.
- **Say no** to friends, events, or activities that drain energy or over stimulate senses.

Flower essences for empaths

In her book, The Sensitive Person's Survival Guide: An Alternative Heath Answer to Emotional Sensitivity & Depression (Ansuz Press, 2001) author Kyra Mesich (www.kyramesich.com) describes her discovery of her empathic sensitivity when she has a sudden depressive episode. She discovers the next day that when her client describes his depressive mania of the previous evening, he was describing her experience exactly, even to the timing of events. This led Mesich to understand the true nature of empathy, which is to be a communication system that we use in a protected, safe manner. Mesich found balance to enjoy the positive aspects of her gift through specific disciplines. Part of her discipline for balance included the following flower essences, a health remedy used for emotional healing and balance.

- *Yarrow rebalances empathy and restores empathic protection.*
- *Pink yarrow are for those empaths who give too much of themselves and need to pull their energy back into balance.*
- *White yarrow is for people who are sensitive to other people's emotions as well as to their environment.*
- *Golden yarrow is helpful for empaths who avoid others and have become shy or introverted to avoid others.*

Explore all flower essences at www.greenhopeessences.com

Creative minds or chaotic minds

Happy creative children smile. Smiles usually accompany calm, confidence, and competence. Children with confidence trust themselves to get through adversity. Calm children know to take a deep breath and watch for a moment before responding. We call it mindfulness or awareness.

The authors' experiences with creative intuitive children who get stressed out is that their minds polarize to two behavioral patterns.

- First, their minds blank out, like withdrawing or dissociating (this is as simple as daydreaming or as earnest as finding a safe place in the mind).

- Second, the pattern, as one adolescent described it, is the mind starts "kicking ass." When you are hurt, distressed, not balanced, or emotionally fragmented, the mind wants to protect you and nags you to "do something."

We are using the term "blank out" to describe what happens to children under distress. Here are some examples of blanking out.

For those under pressure in school, they may stare out the window and daydream. Their mind wanders long distances.

The more intensive pressures, the more a child becomes may dissociate, that is, "goes somewhere else." When a child hears fighting, lives with a consistently alcoholic parent, or is physically or psychologically abused, he finds a safe space for his survival and restoration in his own psyche.

A child's "inside" space can be filled with angels, extraterrestrials, God, invisible friends, or others who help him cope with his reality. That space can also be unsafe if it feels dark, evil, or filled with monsters and other vague and angst-producing creatures.

These "spaces" in the psyche are normal under stressful conditions, and most children recover, which means they know the difference between their "safe space" and reality. Those that do not may experience mental health problems. Consider consultation with a health practitioner if this is the case.

Like your mind, children's minds try to protect them from hurt, pain, or trauma. Another mental stress response may be unconscious psychobabble such as worry, self-blame, and negative self-talk. Some children keep these intense cycles of thoughts inside. Under stress, others cannot hold it in and start to talk it through, sometimes coherently, and sometimes not.

Your attentive listening has healing potential. Empathy and listening give support. Listening to a child's silence, tone of voice, and words gives you clues that a touch on the shoulder or a calming neck massage would calm their minds and bodies. When children talk through, they often find their own solutions without your input.

If worry is common in your creative intuitive's thoughts, bring them to the present moment with your verbal reassurances. Remind them, "You are here, now, and you are safe. Tell me about *now*—how you feel and what you think." The word *now* keeps children focused on the present moment.

Encourage them to describe feelings, thoughts, sensations, and views. Storytelling helps here.

Their minds need to focus on the present and then ask questions in the present tense that spotlight the here. Asking questions this way produces solutions and draws the child back from daydreaming:

- What is real?
- What is happening?
- What is priority?
- What can I do?
- How many different ways can I do it?
- What help do I need?
- Who can help me?

If the mind talks too much and needs quieting, move to a physical exercise. Laugh, smile, take a walk, dance, and breathe deeply to relax. When the body changes focus, the mind follows. The most important rule to model for a creative child is this: *You become what you focus your attention on.*

Chapter Review

- Parents embark on asking questions and finding answers, especially when confronted by situations in which intuitive children are outside the box and nonconforming.
- Dr. Orloff said, "The advice that I would give intuitive parents who know that their children are also intutive is to help them be comfortable in their own skins—to model the intuition in a seamless way."
- All psychic power and intutive sensing need grounding through the body.
- Your attentive listening has healing potential. Empathy and listening give support. When children talk through, they often find their own solutions without your input.

17

Learning to Shift States, Focus, and Connect

There is no logical way to the discovery of these elemental laws. There is only the way of intuition, which is helped by a feeling for the order lying behind the appearance.

—Albert Einstein

Intuitive children are usually sensitive and more easily stressed than other interactive styles. We want empathic children to know how not to take on pain or negativity. If they are moody, they need to learn how to manage their moods. The intuitive creative child also needs to learn to focus. The psychic child is expected to manage states and move between worlds. The spiritual child feels loss without the inner connection.

All these factors for our children's strengths are critical as they enter school, because medications are doled out too liberally and mental health screenings can easily label a 6-year-old as a problem. Any label—whether arising from mental health, education, or social settings—placed on a child will follow him throughout his life.

This chapter has two purposes:

1. To show you how to help children manage their energy of negative thoughts, unproductive emotions, or lack of focus.
2. To show you how to help children shift moods.

Children's emotional and psychic states

Destiny is not a matter of chance, it is a matter of choice. It is not a thing to be waited for, it is a thing to be achieved.

—William Jennings Bryan

Research on the development of emotional competence in North American children shows that "they have a greater likelihood of acting out either in an emotionally overwhelmed, intimidated or defeated fashion, or they externalize their distress and behave aggressively and defiantly toward others."[1] The reason is the mixed messages of Western civilization about emotions: *stand tall, suck it up, prove yourself, be quiet, you can handle it, be still, sit down.*

Such messages drive our sensitive children to find their own paths and lifestyles. Yet, to march to a different drummer in this culture requires courage and confidence with the support of a mentor. As the forerunners of new consciousness, their skills can't be just good; their skills need to be superb. Self-management skills enable them to find the passion and self-confidence needed for their success. Emotional expression includes speaking, drawing, painting, journaling, exercise, and movement. Emotional management methods include creative drama, music, imagery, story telling, healing touch, breathing and meditation. Researchers have found that emotions communicate to the organs and systems of the body, especially the immune system. Positive emotions produce a beneficial biochemistry; negative emotions trigger a stressful one. Blocked expression or emotional constriction minimizes beneficial communication.

Expressing emotions moves the blocked, suppressed feelings. The movement of emotional energy balances the neuropeptide-receptor network. The reason that consciousness breathing is the optimal method of moving energy is because it:

- Bypasses the need for words.

- Deepens directly to the intent of expression.

- Penetrates to the cellular level where constriction originates.

No, we don't want to shelter children from life. Yet, we have to help them stretch without breaking, learn from their mistakes, and hold the tension when necessary. The strategies in this chapter come from decades of combined experiences of doctors, educators, parents, massage therapists, chiropractors, and psychologists and used by persons trained under or associated with Caron Goode and Tom Goode, ND. All strategies are based on sound science and sane living for sensitive people in a stressed world.

With respect to intuitive children, Full Wave breathing has five goals for all children with intuitive intelligence.

1. To help them become aware of their moods and feelings.

2. To help them find inner strength to manage emotions and face any fear.

3. To help them shift from what distresses them to optimism, calm, or centering that serves their situation, intention, or goals.

4. To help them open their intuition and be self-aware.

5. To enable them to maintain their spiritual connection.

The reason this strategy is so effective is that it brings immediate changes in the biochemistry of the body rather than a having child fighting with emotions, struggling to release a block or insisting that an active mind quit being negative.

Your breath is the key to vitality, inspiration, and connection.

Full Wave breathing

Dr. Tom Goode (*www.InternationalBreathInstitute.com*) is the pioneer behind the Full Wave Breathing movement. Dr. Goode provides breath retraining as the first and single most important exercise.

The exercise called Full Wave breathing returns us to our natural flow or rhythm of breath, much like infants and toddlers in a relaxed state. Their inhale expands the abdomen, rounding it outward slightly, with no pause between inhale and exhale. Breathing into the abdomen is the basic breath movement in Pilates, some yoga exercises, martial arts training, and Full Wave breathing. Full Wave breathing is designed to offset shallow stress-producing breathing in the chest that is now found in children as early as first grade.

Six-year-old Josh, who joined a his classmates on the carpet for their daily breathing circle after recess, said he wanted to share something he learned about breath—that people can't breathe into their gut or abdomen. His illustrated anatomy book at home said we only breathe with our lungs.

His teacher explained that the lungs were attached to a diaphragm muscle below the lungs. Then she pulled from their bookshelf a book about martial arts and shared the picture of the young student breathing into his abdomen to strengthen his vitality. Josh decided he could do that, and the children finished their "quiet" exercise, 10 minutes of Full Wave breathing, before moving into math.

The abdomen is our center of gravity or balance. It's the center of energy and vitality center from which many martial arts postures and moves are begun. Initiating breath from this center, we are energizing and balancing the body. The first step in learning to breathe more effectively is to help children understand that their bodies breathe, that there is a better way to do it, and that they can control it. Breath control is their key to management.

Once your child has grasped the basics of deeper breathing as a tool for staying healthy, calming the mind and body and managing tension and intense emotion, develop an exercise time together. As both of you practice the ease of deeper breathing, you'll be astonished at how connected to each other you feel. Peace will pervade your household. Remind your child, "We feed the body when it's hungry, exercise to make it strong, and breathe to relieve stress, feel our best, and keep our intuitive channels clear.

Breathing benefits intuitive intelligence
- *Conscious or mindful breathing centers children.*
- *Full Wave breathing opens the door to intuition and for spiritual connection. Breath becomes the tool for connecting the inner world with the outer world.*

- *Practicing these breathing techniques retrain and strengthen muscles. The mind and body adapt to having more fuel and vitality.*

- *Within 30 days of several practice sessions a week, children can learn these breathing exercises and experience the health and relaxation benefits they bring, and gain an effective stress management tool.*

- *The Full Wave breath produces relaxation for stressed, high-strung, or creative intellectual temperaments.*

- *Students who sit all day with little exercise or those who need to build vitality and stamina can use 10 minutes of the Full Wave breath, inhaling through the mouth to restore energy.*

- *Use the Full Wave Breath as an isometric exercise for tightening the abdominal and stomach muscles. Exhale and hold the abdomen and the diaphragm muscles taut for 10 seconds. Repeat five to 20 times daily.*

- *Breathe 10 Full Wave breath.*

- *Starting a test, homework, or other focused task. Any task requiring mental or psychic focus.*

Full Wave breathing consists of three easy steps, which involve three body sections: the lower abdomen, solar plexus, and chest.

- Expand the belly on the inhale, pushing it outward gently. Opening the abdomen sparks the gut brain and the instinctual level of intuition.

- Expanding the breath carries it into the solar plexus and into the chest. When your lungs and heart are expanded, you feel your intuitive intelligence as fully alive!

- The exhale is a gentle release, not forced.

By directing your breath, you calm your emotions, lower your blood pressure, and quiet your mind. There is no substitute for sitting quietly and breathing if you want to feel connected to life and energized in your activities throughout your day.

Children can start breath retraining at ages 5 to 7 because by that time, they have become shallow breathers, that is, breathing up into the chest. Shallow breathing produces stress, and most of us shut down our lower breathing by the time we start school.

Step 1: Abdominal breathing

Full Wave Breathing consist of breathing a full, connected breath, with a long inhale and a relaxed exhale. The recommended form of deep abdominal breathing consists of inhaling deeply and slowly through your mouth and expanding the abdomen as you practice. Parents should master the simple steps before teaching their children. Model this breath and show it to a group of intuitive children and you'll find their enthusiasm infectious.

- Place your hand on their abdomen, identifying the area that will expand on the inhale.

or

- Ask your child to place their hand on the abdomen while breathing.
- Start breathing together with an open mouth.
- Expand the belly during inhale.
- Have the child exhale all at once and relax completely.

Continuing with a slow and rhythmic pace, start the inhale again. This continuous breath is a relaxed way to bring oxygen into the body. You can help by expanding your touch on an inhale and pushing the abdomen gently inward on the exhale. Intuitive children should excel in this step one of breath retraining before going to step two. This step alone can decrease excitation levels and bring calm.

Practice for brief periods of time, allowing your child to exercise the abdominal muscles. Practice together until your child can comfortably extend the abdomen on inhaling. Then, practice the complete exhale and fully relax. You may stay with this for 10 minutes, through several sessions or during a period of weeks, until you and your child breathe into the abdomen easily and without strain. Play music to breathe by and use gentle touch for deeper relaxation.

Figure 1

Benefits of abdominal breathing

Relaxation: Breathe in deeply and slowly through your mouth and expanding the abdomen as you practice. Visualize the air traveling right down to your abdomen and say the word relax *to yourself as you breathe in. Then breathe out slowly and gently through your mouth. As you exhale, imagine the stress and tension leaving your body with your breath and think the word "calm." Deliberately let your muscles become soft as you exhale. Take three deep breaths at a time in one set.*

Activates intuition: Within the abdomen resides the gut's brain or the "enteric nervous system," which is located in the sheaths of tissue lining the esophagus, stomach, small intestine and colon. The gut's brain plays a major role in human happiness and misery. Many gastrointestinal disorders like colitis and irritable bowel syndrome originate from problems within the gut's brain. Also the instinctual intuition triggers butterflies, flutters, and its sensation alerts us.

> ***Activates metabolism:*** *This specific exercise has metabolic benefits for overweight children and adults. Overweight individuals find their breathing and heart affected by the state of their body. They may have a breathing disorder related to cardiovascular problems. One of the common reasons for the heart problems is that overweight individuals are often inactive and do not give themselves a chance to strengthen their heart muscle.*

Step 2: Breathe into the solar plexus

The solar plexus is the place below your chest, but above your abdomen. The term *solar plexus* names a network of nerves, located in the stomach area, which connects to all our internal organs. The solar plexus is an important nerve reception and transmission area. Some people believe the solar plexus processes emotional and energetic stimuli. Through the solar plexus, we directly access our intuition and connect with our inner resources. Through the solar plexus, region of digestion, we come to understand what we can and cannot digest in regard to emotional sensitivity and empathic ability.

The second step of Full Wave breathing brings the breath from the abdomen into the solar plexus. Children can place their hands around the lower rib cage to feel their breathing muscles move. During inhale, they first breathe into the abdomen, and then expand into the solar plexus. The breathing also expands the lower ribs and exercises the diaphragm and intercostal muscles.

Inhale through the mouth, expand the abdomen (step one), then expand or pull the breath into the solar plexus. The lower rib cage automatically expands. Exhale fully, relaxing and deflating the entire area. Breathing continuously, inhale again, following the same pattern. Note that on the exhale, the abdomen and solar plexus deflate naturally with the exhale. There is no need to force it or try to make it happen. Rather, just observe that it does happen.

Use your intuition to help children understand how to move the breath up through their bodies in expanding their rib cage. Action verbs such as *move up, expand, pull up, and lift* have different connotations for children, and they may not understand what action you want them to take. Demonstration works! You might ask the children, "What word best describes moving

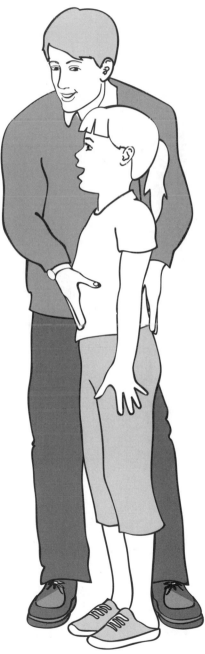

Figure 2

your breath from here (abdomen) to here (solar plexus)?" The metaphor we like best is that of a wave. You can ask children to practice moving the wave through their body.

Another way to teach moving the breath from the abdomen into the solar plexus is the two-stroke breath. Here's how it works.

On stroke or count one, inhale deeply into the abdomen.

On count two of the inhale, move the breath into the solar plexus.

Exhale smoothly, and repeat the two-stroke breath.

This two-stroke breath can be done lying or sitting. Children enjoy breathing to music so they can keep count of the two strokes. (Try the "Cosmic Waltz" offered by the International Breath Institute.) As your child's breath coach, clap or tap the rhythm to help her establish a pattern.

Step 3: Into the chest

Next the breath moves into your chest, the heart center. According to research, the heart receives and responds to intuition first, before sending further information to the brain.[1] The third step of the Full

Wave Breath is to expand the breath into the chest from the solar plexus and abdomen. At this point, the Full Wave Breath truly becomes like a wave that starts in the belly and moves up through the chest. The three separate steps of the Full Wave Breath becomes a smooth flow of breathing.

As you did when teaching the previous steps, show your child the flow of breath by placing your hand on the abdomen, solar plexus, and then the chest. Practice breathing from the abdomen and expanding into the chest. Help your child orient to his chest by placing your palm there as he breathes. Show him the fullness of the abdomen while inhaling and move the fullness from the abdomen all the way into the chest. Emphasize the wave-like movement.

Case studies link shallow breathing with a battery of physical and

Figure 3

emotional disorders and psychosomatic illnesses. Using Full Wave breathing, you can give adolescents a tool to use during times of stress, thus helping to prevent emotional and behavior-related illness. Working with your child in this manner helps to expand the safety and trust in your personal relationship. It makes it easier for your and your child to talk about and define adolescent dreams and intentions, make the best choices,,,, and live a positive lifestyle.

Full Wave breathing opens the inner doorways of clear thinking, intuition, and awareness so your intuitive child or teen can clarify values and goals, experience the feeling of joyful calm, and then act affirmatively. Another result of Full Wave Breathing is that all the organs and body systems harmonize, pulse in one rhythm, from the brain to the toes.

Heart-to-heart resonance

Your time is limited, so don't waste it living someone else's life. Don't be trapped by dogma—which is living with the results of other people's thinking. Don't let the noise of other's opinions drown out your own inner voice. And most important, have the courage to follow your heart and intuition. They somehow already know what you truly want to become. Everything else is secondary.

—Steve Jobs

For an intuitive child to feel comfortable shifting moods and trusting their intuitive intelligence, love is an absolute ingredient. You transfer love through your hands when you touch, through your hugs, though your eye gazing, and through your voice and expression.

We mentioned previously in the book that our heartbeats entrain into one rhythm when connected. Heart-to-heart hugs synchronize body rhythms and establishes resonance between people. We think of resonance as a peaceful response to each other, calming to emotions and clearing of thoughts. The hug is one of several methods for creating energy harmony within one's self or with another. Resonance is established when two people touch each other's hearts.

Soft eye contact for a long gaze register on brain-mapping images as pleasure.

Figure 4

Placing your hand on your heart and\or your child's heart while breathing into the abdomen, as in the full wave breath quickly creates resonance. Completing the Full Wave breath with the resonance of intention instantly creates connection. Note in Figure 4 that full-bodied hug aligns the hearts intentionally.

Also for toddlers and children, resonance can be easily established. Note in Figure 5 how the mother, who holds the toddler in her lap, is inhaling and expanding the abdomen synchronizing the child's breathing to her own. Like the heartbeat, the rhythm of breath also harmonizes the rhythms of the mind and body.

Researchers have found that positive emotions exert corresponding feelings on the organs and systems of the body, especially the immune system. What greater gift can we provide for empaths, psychics,

creatives, and spiritually attuned children than to help
them maintain the connection
to calm coherence within and
without?

Use this exercise to see
what your inner wisdom has
to say, see how you specifically
communicate with yourself,
practice our communication
skills, and practice our interpretation skills.

With closed or open eyes,
practice Full Wave breathing for
five to ten minutes for deep relaxation. Starting at the top of
your head and moving to the
tips of your toes (or you can
reverse the process), scan your
body for feelings that want to
communicate with you.

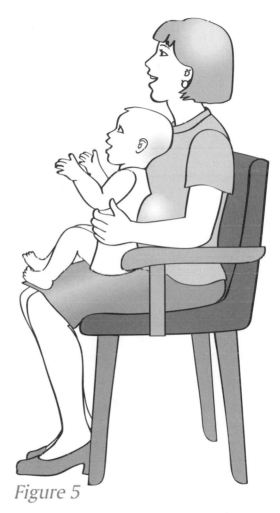

1. Choose one feeling.
2. Place your hand over
   the location of the
   feeling.

Figure 5

3. Ask the following
   questions and respond with the first thing that you are aware
   of: *What I call this feeling is...? Another name for this feeling
   that would be more helpful to me is...? What this feeling is saying
   is...? What do you want me to do with this information? Do I
   need to take an action?*

The joy of this exercise is that the body always responds. The exercise
strengthens an intuitive's ability to hear, know, or see—become aware—of
what the body communicates.

Meditation

Meditation reorients the brain from anxiety to calmness, reducing cortisol and other stress hormone levels. Mechanically, meditation is the creation of a relaxed mental state.

Harvard Professor, Herbert Benson, MD, documented the positive effects of the relaxation response in a book with the same name. He details the benefits of the profound relaxation achieved as the brain wave pattern shifted from Beta (12–30cps) to Alpha (8–11cps).

The meditative state, similar to states of prayerfulness or contemplation, open to the child-like states. These states are not of innocence, but states of knowing and connection. Remember, the toddlers' and preschoolers' brain wave states are in this relaxed, yet alert state, where the intuitive intelligence is peak.

Full Wave Breathing also produces an alpha brain wave pattern with no movement or mantra. Ten minutes of deeper breathing for relaxation and then sitting in the stillness and calm is a very pleasant meditation.

The mindfulness meditation exercise is the practice of sitting and watching your breathing. As you focus on your breathing, thoughts come and go. If you become distracted by any thought, you just return your awareness to your breathing.

Chapter Review

- As the forerunners of new consciousness, our children's skills need to be superb.
- Self-management skills enable children with intuitive intelligence to find the passion and self-confidence needed for their success.
- The exercise called Full Wave breathing returns us to our natural flow or rhythm of breath, much like infants and toddlers in a relaxed state.

- Full Wave breathing is designed to offset shallow stress-producing breathing in the chest that is now found in children as early as first grade.

- Full Wave breathing consists of three easy steps, which involve three body sections: lower abdomen, solar plexus, and chest. Expand the belly on the inhale, pushing it outward gently. Opening the abdomen sparks the gut brain and the instinctual level of intuition. The exhale is a gentle release, not forced.

- Full Wave breathing opens the inner doorways of clear thinking, intuition, and awareness, so your intuitive child or teen can clarify values and goals, experience the feeling of joyful calm, and then act affirmatively.

- Heart-to-heart hugs synchronize body rhythms and establishes resonance between people. We think of resonance as a peaceful response to each other, calming to emotions, and clearing of thoughts.

- Meditation reorients the brain from anxiety to calmness, reducing cortisol and other stress hormone levels. Mechanically, meditation is the creation of a relaxed mental state.

Conclusion

What would it be like if children were given the freedom and support to be who they were born to be? Could we lead our children to create inner harmony and strong connections with others by encouraging their intuitive intelligence to shine through? What if we raised our children and provided them with the tools they need to trust their inner guidance?

The children of today stretch and challenge our learning. Parents of intuitive children need first to commit to the role of parent. We have to direct expressions of inventive and creative thoughts, help empaths deal with emotional overwhelm, establish resilience, and face fears of ghosts. Children with intuitive intelligence, challenged by cultural systems which do not know how to connect with or teach them, need permission to follow their personal path and optimize their talent. We can give that permission and model it for them by developing our intuitive parenting. We also need to become intuitive parents.

Our truest parenting success is the feeling of resonance with our child, the connection of hearts, the meeting of minds—congruence.

This is where commitment to being an intuitive parent becomes our greatest achievement and one we need to make the most important job we will ever have. We no longer have the freedom to treat our children like second class citizens, unworthy of our respect. They not only deserve our respect, but also demand it. Our intuitive children are more in tune to their natural rhythm. They are willing to stand up for things that matter; willing to fight for their beliefs; willing to confront people who aren't being genuine; and they are willing to express their emotions in whatever style is right for their spirits.

In this book, we have shown in detail the differing intuitive intelligences and given you techniques for working with each. We have also shown how intuition is a natural intelligence that all children have the capacity to develop, but they need guidance from us parents to build a strong spiritual foundation.

As committed parents, we have the power to change our world for ourselves and the future of our children. The shift requires a new awareness of what it means to be a parent of an intuitive. For the first time in decades, we awaken to the power and magnificence we all possess. Our children, labeled with terms such as *sensitive, indigo, crystal,* and *special needs*, are waking us up and urging us to step up for them. For the first time ever, we have an abundance of resources, support, and validation for the intuitive nudges we have felt. Let's make this time in history our time. Let's nurture our child's special gifts and those inside us that may be dormant or were unrecognized for generations.

We have been given the special honor and privilege of raising intuitive, enlightened children, and it is our intention to raise awareness for all parents who have been given the same special gift. Welcome to this newest dimension of parenting. May this be the greatest journey you ever take.

May the God within inspire you to fully open your heart, exposing the brilliance of your light, illuminating the path for your children to follow.

Appendix: Renaissance of Intuition

You can't use up creativity. The more you use it, the more you have. Sadly, too often creativity is smothered rather than nurtured. There has to be a climate in which new ways of thinking, perceiving, questioning are encouraged.

—Maya Angelou

Intuition comes of age

Intuition is an essential part of the human mind, which includes our conscious processes and unconscious processes—thought perception, emotion, will, memory, and imagination. Intuition involves nurturing self-awareness of the inner world, the outer world, and the connection in between

We wholeheartedly agree with the *Utne Reader*'s observation that "Intuition is hot."[1] Business schools recognize intuition as a key to creativity and its value in problem solving and decision-making. Recent books such as *Blink* (2005) by Malcolm Gladwell consolidated years of research on intuition to executive decision makers, and *Strategic Intuition* (2007) by William Duggan focused on how creative ideas take place in the practice of business and decision-making. Corporations are even hiring intuitionists for their counsel.

Recognition for the intuitive mind with its way of discovery and knowing has advanced significantly in the last decades. What started with Carl Jung's concept that people have four primary paths for processing information has evolved into the intricacies of brain mapping in the field of neuroscience. We know how we learn, which part of the brain is involved, and how to reprogram patterns that don't work.

The renaissance of intuition has arrived. Let's trace the progress of intuition through the last several decades as it made its way into mainstream thought and awareness. Intuitives have always been here. Only recently has modern society accepted and found intuition useful.

The 1960s

The 1960s was the explosive decade of mind-expanding drug use and led to further investigation of consciousness. The era also introduced regulated studies of LSDs effects and sleep deprivation studies to observe brain wave patterns. Research labs studied the brain's capabilities.

In 1969, the American Association for the Advancement of Science recognized parapsychology as a legitimate scientific field. Humanistic and transpersonal psychologies made great strides in expanding our understanding of human consciousness since intuition was on the fringe in the 1960s and are considered legitimate and accredited sciences.

1970s

The government's interest in psi activities during the Cold War period peaked further interest in intuition. The Stargate Project was established to investigate the military application of psychic research. One of the well-known projects was the remote viewing, which investigated whether psychics could see an event using long-distance clairvoyance. These government projects started in the 1970s and continued through 1995.

Another significant breakthrough in 1972 involved Dr. Roger Sperry, who differentiated the specific functions of the left-brain and the right brain. His groundbreaking work earned him the Nobel Prize and gave a physical basis to the ability to work with images, intuition, and holistic thinking in the right brain hemisphere. Human capacity was explored and brain research provided a biological foundation for intuitive intelligence and thinking.

Further brain research in the 1970s by Dr. Paul MacLean introduced the idea of human brains developing along an evolutionary tract. We don't have one brain; we have a series of interconnected sub-brains, the "triune brain." Each sub-brain displays its own form of intelligence, motor functions, sense of time and specialized tasks.

1. Reptilian brain is the brain stem, so named because it includes structures of a reptile brain and developed five hundred million years ago. It governs vital survival activities like our breathing, heart rate, body temperature, and balance. This brain also gives us the basis for instinct, which we can separate from intuition, as people confuse human instinct with intuitive intelligence.

2. The limbic brain grew in small mammals about 150 million years ago. It governs emotional states and produces emotional memory patterns, which assign values based on cultural and relational influences. This brain developed in response to increasingly complex relationships in mammals.

3. The human neocortex expanded the brain capacity several million years ago and contains the two brain hemispheres. Brain functions included abstract thought, language, and consciousness. Human capacity for learning has grown into the cultures we experience today.

The reptilian brain processes instinctual responses that include the gut brain. Intuition has roots in the gut brain, but is processed in the emotional brain, or the limbic system. The neocortex is the thinking brain, choosing information we should listen to and act on from the reservoir of our memory. Intuition involves the interplay between the limbic system and the neocortex. The right hemisphere has richer neural connections to the limbic system than does the left, and it draws information and perceptions from time and space. This is how we make sense of our world.

So how do we make sense of intuitive intelligence within our world?

Intuitive intelligence

Our logical mind addresses stable patterns, snapshots of reality stored in our memory banks, for the practical living. The holistic or holographic side of our reality, intuitive intelligence comes from within. By focusing our attention on *how* intuition presents, we act from deeper understanding.

Here is the story of how intuitive intelligence has grown, along with the advances in brain science and information processing.

1980s

In 1983, a Harvard Education professor, Howard Gardner, proposed a theory of seven intelligences to explain a broad range of human aptitudes. Gardner has defined intelligence as "the capacity to solve problems or to fashion products that are valued in one or more cultural setting."[2]

The definition implied that intelligence is based on its utility and value within its culture. This was a major breakthrough in education and psychology, moving educators beyond the single intellectual quotient—IQ. The concept of intelligence expanded to value children's talents in broader areas.

In the following list of Gardner's intelligences, schools value linguistics and logic. The arts and sports value spatiality, physical skills, and musical skills. And the interpersonal skills and intrapersonal awareness underlie emotional ability, social skills, and natural intuition.

Gardner's Seven Intelligences:

1. Linguistic intelligence—smart use of words.
2. Logical-mathematical intelligence—gifted use of number reasoning.
3. Spatial intelligence—sharp use of visuals and pictures.
4. Bodily-kinesthetic intelligence—able use of body and physical talents.
5. Musical intelligence—gifted use of lyrics, melodies and rhythms.
6. Interpersonal intelligence—empathic ability with social skills and ability to know and read others.
7. Intrapersonal intelligence—competent awareness of inner feelings and self-reflection.

In the years since Gardner's identified intelligences, he has considered adding more. *Naturalist intelligence* is being smart about or attuned to nature and experiences in natural world. *Spiritual intelligence* is an exploration of the nature of existence. Possibly, Gardner ponders moral intelligence and existential intelligence. Are these intelligences valued by our culture and do they solve problems?

Gardner's model of intelligences broke the hold of the single intelligent quotient (IQ) by which children were compared for decades in education. Gardner's work gave credence to the experience of the classroom teachers who always saw children's unique gifts.

In Gardner's model, the natural intuitive intelligence can be viewed in interpersonal skills like empathy, intrapersonal skills, self-awareness, or naturalist intelligence.

Intelligence is broader and more flexible than past educationalists and psychologists have assumed.

The late 1980s and early 1990s brought an explosion of religious, spiritual, and dream experiences. People experienced the "nonphysical world" in myriad ways:

- Contact with extraterrestrials.
- Shaktiput from gurus.
- Personal experiences with angels, Jesus, and other nonphysical entities.
- The mind-expanding drug experiences of the 1960s became "other-worldly" experiences of the 1980s and 1990s. These developments help us better understand our intuitive and spiritual experiences.

1990s

In 1995, when *Emotional Intelligence* hit the bookstores, the establishment woke up to value of their limbic systems. For example, popularity for a high emotional quotient (EQ) gained value over intellectual prowess in the workplace and in schools. Intuition became a competency, one of the emotional intelligence skills.

Intuition and gut feeling register awareness: identifying emotions, knowing how we are affected by emotions, and our ability to use them for our well-being—including our ability to learn self-correction from our mistakes.

Intuitive intelligence, viewed in its own right, is broader than can be defined by emotional intelligence. Emotions are inaccurate gauges and differ from intuitions, gut feelings, or other somatic awareness. As Dr. Robert Flower, author of *The Exceptional Mind* (2008) and founder of the Gilchrist Institute explained, "Emotions are your feelings, and intuitions are your sensing. Emotions will lie to you and intuitions are more valid, but we don't trust them fully. My research confirms that trusting intuitive intelligence correlates with less emotional issues.

"I have three children. They're all in there 30s now, in business and they all do very well. My wife and I always tried to develop their intuition. We would play games with them to force their intuition. We would get them to trust what they saw and felt. Their intuitive exercises gave them a tremendous amount of strength in their lives.

"The natural model of intelligences is infallible, however we have followed educational, psychological, empirical models which are false constructions that our children must fit into, like using the one standard IQ for 40 years. The natural model is a personable model where children's gifts can be identified and nurtured."

Because the word *intuition* derives from Latin *intueri*, which means "to look within," Gardner's definition is helpful, yet limited. Goleman's work in emotional intelligence includes strata of intuitive processing. Like any of the natural intelligences, intuition is a vast continuum and a variety of expressions from artistry to psychic skills.

In today's world, we focus on the child's natural core genius. Intuitive intelligence is part of children's core genius. This natural intelligence can grow into a unique talent. Children with intuitive intelligence are ready to take their place in the world. Our job as parents and coaches is to assist them.

Notes

Introduction

1. McCraty, Rollin, PhD, et al. "Electrophysiological Evidence of Intuition: Part 1. The Surprising Role of the Heart." *The Journal of Alternative and Complementary Medicine.* 10 (2004): 133–143.

Chapter 8

1. "Our Toxic World." *High Tech Health.* (2005) *www.hightechhealth.com/html/toxic_world.htm*

2. Ibid.

3. "Our Children at Risk: The 5 Worst Environmental Threats to Their Health." *Natural Resources Defense Council.* (Nov. 1997) *www.nrdc.org/health/kids/ocar/ocarinx.asp*

4. "Our Toxic World." *High Tech Health.* (2005) *www.hightechhealth.com/html/toxic_world.htm*

5. Crain, MD, PhD, Ellen F. "Environmental Threats to Children's Health: A Challenge for Pediatrics." *Ambulatory Pediatric Association (APA), Presidential Address."* Ambulatory Pediatric Association. (May 15, 2000).

6. "Our Children at Risk: The 5 Worst Environmental Threats to Their Health." *Natural Resources Defense Council* (Nov. 1997).

7. Sheppard, Jane. "Growing Up on Chemicals—Our Children's Toxic Environment." *Healthy Child. www.healthychild.com/childrens-toxic-environment.htm*

8. Sheppard, Jane. "Growing Up on Chemicals — Our Children's Toxic Environment." *Healthy Child.* *http://www.healthychild.com/childrens-toxic-environment.htm*

9. Suzelis, Ted, ND. "Protecting Your Family from Environmental Toxicity." *Ohio Naturopathic.* *www.ohionaturopathic.com/articles/environmental%20toxicity.pdf*

10. Gilbert, Sue. "Backyard Barbequing: Harmful to Your Health?" *Your Total Health.* *http://yourtotalhealth.ivillage.com/backyard-barbeque-harmful-your-health.html.*

11. Jemmott, Janet M. "Bottled Water vs. Tap Water." *Reader's Digest.* (Feb. 2008). *www.rd.com/your-america-inspiring-people-and-stories/rethink-what-you-drink/article51807.html*

12. Francis M. Pottenger, MD. Research. *Price-Pottenger Nutrition Foundation.* *www.ppnf.org/catalog/ppnf/pottengerresearch.htm*

Chapter 9

1. "Our Children at Risk: The 5 Worst Environmental Threats to Their Health." *Natural Resources Defense Council.* (Nov. 1997).

2. Ibid.

3. Ibid.

4. *Schab D.W., et al. Journal of-Dev Behavior Pediatric.* (2004) 25: 423–434

Chapter 10

1. Hammond, B. "Leading and Learning." *http://leading-learning.blogspot.com/2006/11/creating-environment-to-nurture.html*

2. Rusch, E. *Generation Fix: Young Ideas for a Better World.* Oregon: Beyond Words Publishing, (2002).

3. Policastro. "Creative Intuition: An Integrative Review." Creativity Research Journal. 8 (1995): 99–113.

4. Berns, G. "Neuroscience Sheds New Light on Creativity." Fast Company, 129 (October, 2008).

5. Bouchez, C. "Understanding ADHD and the Creative Child." Health Feature. *www.MedicineNet.com.*

6. Ibid.

7. Policastro, E. "Creative Intuition: An Integrative Review. Creativity Research Journal. 8 (1995) 99–113.

Chapter 11

1. Goldberg, EH. *A Guide to Promoting Resilience in Children: Strengthening the Human Spirit.* The International Resilience Project, part of the *Early Childhood Development: Practice & Reflection* series. Bernard Van Leer Foundation. *http://resilnet.uiuc.edu/library/grotb95b.html*

2. Ibid

3. *www.heartmath.org*

Chapter 13

1. Vaughan, F. "What is spiritual intelligence?" *Journal of Humanistic Psychology.* 42 (2002): 16–33.

Chapter 14

1. Reprinted with permission "The Religious and Other Beliefs of Americans." The Harris Poll #119 (November 29, 2007). © 2007 HarrisIneractive. *www.harrisinteractive.com/harris_poll/index.asp?PID=838*

2. Bazelson, E. "A Question of Resilience." *The New York Times Magazine.* (April 2006.)

Chapter 15

1. Aron, E. *The Highly Sensitive Child, Helping Our Children Thrive When the World Overwhelms Them.* Broadway; 1 edition (October 8, 2002) P. 7.

2. Woulfe, Rebecca of *www.childhoodmatters.com*. "Experiencing Emotions," Parenting with Passion column, at *www.inspiredparenting.net.*

Chapter 16

1. Atwater, P.M.H., "Indigo Children: Fact or Fiction?" in column *Young Psychics* at *www.globalpsychics.com.*

Chapter 17

1. Sammi, C. and R. Thompson. *The Development of Emotional Competence,* New York: Guilford Press, 1999.

Appendix

1. B. Naparstek. "Extrasensory Etiquette, when intuition hits, what next. *Utne Reader.*

2. Gardner, H. and T. Hatch. "Multiple intelligences go to school: Educational implications of the theory of multiple intelligences." *Educational Researcher.* 18 (1989): 4–9.

Index

About the Authors

Dr. Caron B. Goode, NCC, DAPA, assists people to effect lasting transformation through her spiritual coaching, books, inspirational speaking, and seminars. The author of 10 books, Caron is a source of inspiration for those who want to make a difference. The common thread of her work in education, counseling, wellness, and spirituality is the mind-body-spirit connection. She is an expert in how to access it, bring it into focus, and put it into successful action.

Caron has combined her considerable professional endeavors into an educational program for training and certifying parents and professionals in supporting families. She champions parent coaching and leading-edge parent education. She has positioned the Academy for Coaching Parents International (*www.acpi.biz*) at the forefront of the parent coaching movement to support connection and empowerment. For this work, she received the Mom's Choice Lightworker of the Year award in 2008. Her coaching for parents columns touch hundreds of thousands of people monthly. Her most recent books are *Help Kids Cope with Stress and Trauma,* and *The Art and Science of Coaching Parents.*

Caron also manages *www.inspiredparenting.net,* which provides strategies for parenting the whole child. This site supports children's physical health, emotional fluency, mental development, and spiritual enrichment. Information on classes and training in working with intuitive children can be found at *www.academyforcoachingparents.com/ici/classes.htm.*

Tara Paterson, ACPI, CCPI, has been building bridges with moms and families for many years. Her passion first revealed itself with JustforMom.com, a Website business with advice, ideas, and resources designed to "touch each Mom's life, one Mom at a time." She went on to create Moms In Print, the Just For Mom foundation and the prestigious Mom's Choice Awards®; and has been the recipient of a portion of the proceeds from the Chicken Soup series—*Chicken Soup for the Mother and Son Soul.*

Tara received her parent coach certification through the Academy for Coaching Parents International and is currently the only one with an accreditation for Coaching Parents with Intuitives; is a trainer for the Academy in the specialty niche Parenting Intuitive Children; and is a nationally syndicated columnist for American Chronicle newspapers and the online publication Children of the New Earth. She is the spokesperson for the Mom's Choice Awards and is an expert blogger for the Partnership for a Drug Free America and Cynergreen. She has also been a spokesperson for Glade, Hidden Valley, and SuperPages.com.

Tara was nominated as the 2002 Entrepreneur of the Year by the Loudoun County Chamber of Commerce, and was awarded Entrepreneur of the Year in 2003 by a Northern Virginia networking group. She has also been seen on CNN, *The Today Show,* the *Early Show,* 48 Hours, and has been featured in the *Washington Post, Newsweek,* the *Purcellville Gazette,* the *Loudoun Magazine* and quoted in the *USA Today* and *Parenting Magazine.*

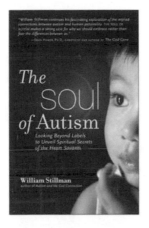
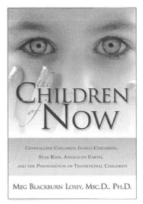
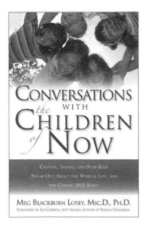